MISSO

Off the Beaten Path

"Uncovers the rich diversity of the Show Me State."
—*Allstate Adventures*

"Even for a native, the book gives a hankering to jump in the car and go off to explore."
—*The Springfield* (MO) *News-Leader*

MISSOURI
Off the Beaten Path™

Second Edition

by
Cathy Johnson
and Patti DeLano

A Voyager Book

The Globe Pequot Press

Old Saybrook, Connecticut

Cover and text illustrations by Cathy Johnson
Cover: Octagonal schoolhouse at Watkins Woolen Mill State Historic Site

Off the Beaten Path is a trademark of The Globe Pequot Press, Inc.

Library of Congress Cataloging-in-Publication Data

Johnson, Cathy (Cathy A.)
Missouri : off the beaten path / by Cathy Johnson and Patti DeLano. — 2nd ed.
    p.   cm
  "A Voyager book."
  Includes index.
  ISBN 1-56440-161-8
  1. Missouri—Guidebooks.   I. DeLano, Patti.   II. Title.
F464.3.J64   1993
917.7804'43—dc20   92-31220
                                                        CIP

Manufactured in the United States of America
Second Edition/First Printing

To a friendship that withstood co-authorship;
to our fellow travelers Bob and Chris, and Harris;
and to Missouri—the Heart of America
and a great place to live.

About the Authors

Born in Independence, Missouri, naturalist, artist, and writer Cathy Johnson has always loved the backroads. She and her husband, previously keepers of a twenty-acre farm, now live in a small Victorian home on the edge of town in Excelsior Springs, Missouri, where Cathy serves on the arts council, Main Action Group, the board of the Good Samaritan Center, and the citizens advisory board of the Watkins Mill Camp for Boys, a Missouri Division of Youth Services facility. She was chosen Conservation Communicator of the Year by the Burroughs Audubon Society in 1987, won the AAUW's Thorpe Menn award for Literary Achievement, and is included in *Who's Who in the Midwest.*

A contributing editor with a regular monthly column for *The Artist's Magazine,* Cathy also writes and illustrates natural history pieces for *Country Living.* Her previously published books include *The Local Wilderness, Painting Nature's Details in Watercolor, Watercolor Tricks and Techniques, Drawing and Painting from Nature, The Wild Foods Cookbook, The Nocturnal Naturalist* (published by The Globe Pequot Press), *Sketching in Nature, On Becoming Lost, Creating Textures in Watercolor, One Square Mile,* and *The Naturalist's Cabin,* which chronicles the building of her cabin studio/retreat on an eighteen-acre plot of woodland in Excelsior Springs.

Missouri native Patti DeLano has been traveling the globe since she was twenty. A flight attendant for Trans World Airlines for ten years, she gave up flying to raise a family. She and her husband, Bob, a pilot for TWA, travel extensively. Their youngest son, Chris, attends the University of Missouri.

Patti was mayor of Excelsior Springs and was on the city council for six years. As a member of the board of directors of the Missouri Municipal League, she traveled throughout Missouri, meeting people from towns and cities across the state. She currently writes a weekly column for the *Daily Standard* in Excelsior Springs, where she has also worked as a reporter. Patti's second book, *Kansas: Off the Beaten Path* (coauthored by Cathy Johnson), and third book, *Arkansas: Off the Beaten Path,* have also been published by The Globe Pequot Press. She is now working on a novel based on the 1864 journal of a woman on the Oregon Trail.

Contents

Acknowledgments

No book comes easily, but a sense of humor helps. It's especially true of a book of this sort, which requires so many hours of research and fine-tuning. The Missouri Tourism Bureau and the Missouri departments of Conservation and Natural Resources, not to mention all the visitors' bureaus and chambers of commerce we contacted in hundreds of little towns, made it easier. We want to offer special thanks to Pete Rucker and to all those— too numerous to mention by name—on our mailing lists who came through with letters full of ideas and inspirations; thanks also to Shirley Graff and John and Sally Randazzo for offering their services as proofreaders with opinions.

It's impossible to include all the wonderful, quirky places we discovered in the course of researching this book—it would weigh five pounds. Others we simply did not know about; still others have recently appeared or, sadly, have gone out of business. If you know of a special place, or a change in an existing listing, please write the publishers so that we can add this information when we next update the book.

Introduction

Think of Missouri and a hundred images tumble forward like candy from a piñata. The Pony Express. The Santa Fe Trail. Lewis and Clark. The Civil War. Frank and Jesse James. Mark Twain (who once said that he was born here because "Missouri was an unknown new state and needed attractions"; we certainly got one in Samuel Clemens).

But all of the images are not from the distant past, flickering like a silent movie through the veil of time. There's Branson, now threatening Nashville as the country music capital of the country, with twenty-seven theaters and stars of the magnitude of Johnny Cash and Andy Williams. (We'll tell you how to beat the crowds and traffic and help you find a quiet B&B instead of a computer-located motel.) There's also the Plaza, the world's first shopping center. Kansas City steaks. Charlie Parker, and jazz. General John J. Pershing. The Gateway Arch. Barbecue. Writers Calvin Trillin and Richard Rhodes. Actors Kathleen Turner, Bob Cummings, John Goodman, and Don Johnson, as well as Walt Disney, all have ties to Missouri. And of course, our own Harry S Truman. Now you're on a roll.

What you may *not* think of immediately are the things we will show you in *Missouri: Off the Beaten Path*. Did you know that J. C. Penney got his start here? There's a museum to honor his modest beginnings in Hamilton. And Jacques Cousteau—when you think of the man, you imagine oceanic dives in faraway places, right? Not always. Cousteau filmed a "deep-earth dive" right here in Bonne Terre and explored his way up the Mississippi and Missouri rivers as well. Then there's the Kingdom of Callaway, with its postwar ties to none other than Winston Churchill. There are wineries and breweries and distilleries, and there are elegant restaurants and comfort-food cafes that range from fine French to fire-breathing Cajun, with home style cooking settled somewhere in between.

What we are *not* is flat farmland, empty prairie, or wall-to-wall cows (or cowboys and Indians, for that matter). There's a rich diversity of landscape here.

Missouri is covered with forests and rolling hills. It boasts over 5,000 caves and those are only the ones we know about. The rugged white bluffs along the rivers (the rocky remains of a prehistoric inland sea) and the volcanic formations and karst sinks in the Lake of the Ozarks area are among the most beautiful in the country. The rivers that sculpted all this spectacular scenery are magnets for exploration; the Jacks Fork, the Eleven Point, and the Current rivers are designated National Scenic Riverways. Remnant prairies still beckon—patchwork bits and pieces left over from presettlement days, when the big bluestem and gayfeather were tall enough to hide a man on horseback, and the wind-driven waves imitated a sea of grass.

The Mississippi River, which forms the eastern boundary of the state, is still one of the busiest shipping lanes in the world, and has been flowing here since before the dawn of time. The upstart Missouri River, on the other hand, was the gift of a departing glacier a short half million years ago; it simply wasn't there before that time. The division between the glaciated plains to the north (rolling and covered with a generous layer of top-soil, also a legacy of the wall of ice, which stole the soil from points north) and the bony Ozark region to the south (rough and hilly with valleys cut deep into rock) is the river that bisects the state from Kansas City to St. Louis. Missouri is where old prairie runs up against the oldest mountain range in the country—a fitting symbol for one of the most historically divided states in the Union.

It was in Missouri that the Civil War was most brutal, issuing as it did from tension that had been building for decades. This pre–Civil War strife between free-state Kansas and the Southern-leaning Missouri was bloody, especially since many Missourians believed that slavery was wrong and worked with the Underground Railroad to help slaves to freedom.

After the Civil War, Quantrill's Raiders and such legendary outlaws as Cole Younger and the James brothers continued the bloodshed. The state bears the reminders to this day. Civil War battlefields and tiny cemeteries, with their solemn testimony of the losses of the war, embody the lingering dichotomy between Northern and Southern sensibilities.

Before the Civil War and for some years afterward, the two rivers—the Missouri and the Mississippi—were main arteries of commerce. All of Missouri's large cities began as river ports with a lively competition between them for business and settlers. Kansas City and its popular hot spot, Westport (formerly Westport Landing); St. Joseph, Lexington, Boonville, and Jefferson City, the capital; and Hermann, Washington, and St. Charles, the first capital, all began as ports on the Missouri. Hannibal, St. Louis, Ste. Genevieve, Cape Girardeau, and New Madrid were ports of call on the Mississippi.

Today the big rivers and their connecting waterway system make a 22,000-mile navigable network. Almost all year the tugs and barges can be seen wherever public and private docks allow commodities to be moved inexpensively by water. Only winter's ice jams stop the flow of traffic.

Kansas City, Missouri's second-largest city (now outgrowing St. Louis, much to the pride of the western part of the state), had its beginnings as a shipping point on the Kansas (called the Kaw) River bend of the Muddy Mo, where the river turns sharply east on its trek across the state's midriff. The region known by early explorers as the Big Blue Country was occupied by the Kanza (Kansas) Indians, whose name means "people of the south wind." The peaceful Kanza engaged in farming, fishing, and trapping; they were quickly displaced when settlers began to move in.

Missouri was once as far off the beaten path as one could get, the jumping-off point to the trackless West; beyond was the great unknown. You can still see the tracks of the wagon wheels etched deeply into our soils on the Santa Fe, California, and Oregon trails.

Now everything's up-to-date in Kansas City, as the lyrics to a song once told us. A beautifully modern metropolis, Kansas City has more fountains than any city except Rome and more miles of tree-lined boulevards than any other American city. The Nelson-Atkins Museum of Art owns one of the finest collections of Oriental art in the country.

St. Louis, on the other side of the state, has a world-class botanical garden and a rich cultural heritage that rivals any big city in the East. Not surprisingly, St. Louis is proud of its French legacy, a gift of the early explorers.

The KATY trail (its name is derived from MKT, the Missouri-Kansas-Texas Railroad) begins nearby in Machens just north of St. Louis. This bicycle and hiking trail follows the old MKT railroad route to Sedalia 90 miles east of Kansas City. By 1994 it will cover 200 miles of river bluffs, forests, and farmlands with cafes and shops along its route to cater to trail buffs.

The word *Missouri* first appeared on maps made by French explorers in the 1600s. It was the name of a group of Indians living near the mouth of a large river. Peketanoui, roughly its Indian name, means "river of the big canoes," and the Missouri would have required them—it was big, swift, and tricky to navigate before the locks and dams of the Corps of Engineers tamed it, or attempted to.

We don't know how the native Americans pronounced Missouri, and it is about a fifty-fifty split among the state's current residents. In a recent survey a little more than half the population, most in western Missouri, pronounced the name "Missour-uh." The eastern half of the state favored "Missour-ee."

The "Show-Me State" carries its nickname proudly. We have a reputation as stubborn individualists, as hardheaded as our own Missouri mules—or so they say—and we won't believe something until you show us. It's not such a bad way to be. Our people, like our agrarian ancestors, want concrete proof—we'll change, all right, but only when we're fully convinced that change is synonymous with progress, and that progress is indeed an improvement. The past is definitely worth preserving when it is as colorful as ours.

So we will show you parts of the Show-Me State that are tucked away off the beaten path. Some are in the middle of farmland, some are in national forests, and some are in our largest cities. There will be no "Worlds of Fun" or "Six Flags Over Mid-America" or Royals' Stadium plugs in this book; these places are definitely *on* the path, and you can find them on your own. What this book does have is something for everyone, as out of the way—and "far from the madding crowd"—as you could wish.

No matter where you're from, whether you love a fine Bordeaux or a fine bourbon, whether you like to go in a sports car, dressed to the nines, or in a pickup truck, wearing an old pair of jeans, you will feel at home in Missouri.

The prices and rates listed in this guidebook were confirmed at press time. We recommend, however, that you call establishments before traveling to obtain current information.

Off the Beaten Path in Southeast Missouri

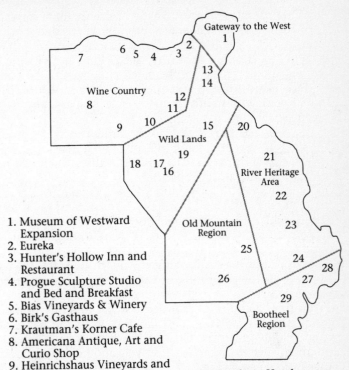

Gateway to the West

Wine Country

Wild Lands

River Heritage Area

Old Mountain Region

Bootheel Region

1. Museum of Westward Expansion
2. Eureka
3. Hunter's Hollow Inn and Restaurant
4. Progue Sculpture Studio and Bed and Breakfast
5. Bias Vineyards & Winery
6. Birk's Gasthaus
7. Krautman's Korner Cafe
8. Americana Antique, Art and Curio Shop
9. Heinrichshaus Vineyards and Winery
10. Onondaga Cave
11. Meramec State Park Lodge
12. Jesse James Wax Museum
13. Mastodon State Park
14. Blue Owl Restaurant and Bakery
15. Bonne Terre Mines
16. Good Ole Days Country Store
17. Johnson Shut-ins
18. Dillard Mill
19. Elephant Rocks State Park
20. Southern Hotel
21. Tric's Family Restaurant
22. Iron Mountain Railway
23. Broussard's Cajun Restaurant
24. Lambert's Cafe
25. Mingo National Wildlife Refuge
26. Margaret Harwell Art Museum
27. Big Oak Tree State Park
28. Towosahgy State Historic Site
29. New Madrid

Southeast Missouri

To call southeast Missouri the most beautiful part of the state wouldn't be fair; beauty is a mysterious commodity based on personal definition, as intangible as smoke. But it has plenty to offer. There is natural beauty—dappled shade of the national forests, cascades of clear blue springs and rivers, and white river bluffs and volcanic rock formations of the Johnson Shut-ins—that meets everyone's definition of beauty. Antebellum and Victorian homes on wide boulevards grace the oldest cities west of the Mississippi. Both beautiful and historic, southeast Missouri will appeal to all your senses with its food, wine, scenery, and rich and varied past.

When the river was the frontier to the American West, thousands crossed it in search of land, freedom, and a new life. Trappers, traders, explorers, and settlers joined Native Americans in the fertile river valleys and rich prairies.

Enter the state from the east, and you will encounter the St. Louis area, the big city/small town that spreads west on Interstate 70 and south on Interstate 55. Sneak off of these two amazingly uncrowded freeways (uncrowded, at least, during non-rush hours) and the many small highways branching off from them to find some of the most charming towns in the state, towns that date back to the beginning of the westward expansion of the country.

Here, you have a choice of crowded festivals and busy public campgrounds or the isolation and peace deep in the national forests and wildlife preserves. Missouri in winter is quietly beautiful and uncrowded; in summer, it is lively and fun. Adventures here range from scuba diving (yes! deep-earth diving in Missouri!) and whitewater canoeing to wine tasting and genealogical searches in the oldest records in the American West. Whether you want to party or to get away from it all, wander off the beaten path into southeast Missouri.

Gateway to the West

The bustling St. Louis area is still the best place to begin westward exploration. Located on a shelf of riverfront under a bluff, the original city spread to the prairies surrounding it. It was the starting point for the Meriwether Lewis and William Clark expedition in 1804. The history of western expansion began here where the Missouri and the Mississippi rivers meet.

St. Louis, founded in 1764, boasts the oldest park west of the Mississippi (Lafayette Park), the second-oldest symphony orchestra in the nation, the world's largest collection of mosaic art at the Cathedral of St. Louis, one of the finest botanical gardens in the world, the futuristic Climatron, and the country's tallest man-made monument, the Gateway Arch, which is also the world's third most popular tourist attraction (but we're talking beaten path here, aren't we?).

It's also a city of firsts. The first Olympiad in the United States was held here in 1904; the first hot dog, ice-cream cone, and iced tea were all introduced at the 1904 World's Fair. Remember "Meet me in St. Louie, Louie, meet me at the fair?"

A great place to start exploring St. Louis is at 1900 Wyoming in historic Benton Park. This building, dating from 1893, now houses a one-stop market that sells anything a traveler might need. You'll find quality merchandise and a complete bed and breakfast reservation service.

One of the finest places to call home in this area is Lemp's Landing in historic Benton Park. This 1893 two-story townhouse is all yours and is popular for visiting CEOs and honeymooners in the St. Louis area. There is a kitchen on the main level, and the second level has bedrooms with king-sized beds and a two-person Jacuzzi. A bottle of champagne and breakfast are included for $125. For information call (314) 771–1993.

If you have come into St. Louis on Amtrak, the **Lafayette House** at 2156 Lafayette Avenue is a good place to stay. The 1876 brick Queen Anne is in historic Lafayette Park and only about a mile from the downtown train depot. This three-story beauty is filled with antiques. Some of the rooms have shared baths, some private baths, and the third-floor suite has its own kitchen. But the convenient location isn't the only reason to choose this spot over a hotel. Hostess Sarah Milligan, a collector of over a thousand cookbooks, will serve the finest breakfast she can create and probably one of the best you will ever find in a B&B. Listen to some of her favorites: San Francisco sourdough chocolate pancakes, cinnamon raisin French toast, scrambled eggs with sweet bell peppers and onions. Lafayette House is also home to a friendly old dog called Mandy and several cats. Rooms run from $50 to $75. There is no sign in the yard because the historical society prohibits it. Call (314) 772–4429 for reservations.

The Gateway Arch may not be exactly off the beaten path—after all, it's one of the most-visited tourist destinations in the country—but did you know there's a wonderful museum tucked away underground *beneath* the Arch in the **Jefferson National Expansion Memorial National Park?** It's the ⊃**Museum of Westward Expansion,** which documents our irrepressible urge to explore and settle lands ever farther westward. We didn't stop until we reached the Pacific Ocean; the museum makes you feel you were along for the trip. You'll see artifacts and displays that relate to the Lewis and Clark expedition, intended not only to find a trade route to the West but to discover the natural history of this new land encompassed by the Louisiana Purchase. You'll find Native American and pioneer artifacts as well, and when you come back out blinking into the sunshine you'll experience a moment of disorientation as you reenter the twentieth century.

The museum is accessible with a $1.00 National Park fee, and it's more than worth the cost (tram fee to the top of the Arch is a bit higher). Also under the Arch are a fine bookstore and gift shop run by the National Park Service; be prepared to take a bit of history home with you.

While you history-minded folk are in the neighborhood of the Arch, don't miss the **Old Cathedral Museum** visible just to the west and still in the Gateway Arch park. Here you'll find some of the finest (and oldest) ecclesiastical art in the country, with works by the Old Masters not uncommon. Documents dating back to the beginning of the Cathedral as well as photographs on the building of the Arch are all part of the museum.

The Old Cathedral Museum (314–231–3250) at 209 Walnut is open daily from 10:00 A.M. till 4:30 P.M.; there is a 25 cent admission charge.

The **Royale Dumpe,** just across from the Arch on First Street, offers dinner theater with a twist. Bawdy humor, sixteenth-century Irish style, is the evening's fare—no nudity, but lots of sexy humor and innuendoes. If you're easily offended—or just blush a lot—this may not be the place for you, but a hearty dinner served during two and a half hours of song, dance, and jokes makes this a fun evening for consenting adults.

Laclede's Landing, just north of the Arch, is the oldest part of St. Louis; the buildings are part of the French Creole heritage of the area, and artist Anna Maria Von Phul may have captured them in watercolor when she visited this area in the early 1800s.

You can see some of the local characters at St. Louis's answer to Madame Tussaud's when you visit **Laclede's Landing Wax Museum** (314–241–1155) at 720 North Second Street daily from 10:00 A.M. to 8:00 P.M. (call for winter hours). You'll find more than 150 life-sized wax effigies (including presidents and kings) authentically costumed and many in settings depicting their historic era. Spooky! Admission is $3.50 for adults and $2.50 for children under twelve.

Still in the downtown area (and the air of the past) is the **St. Louis Mercantile Library Association** at 510 Locust. If you admire the works of Missouri artist George Caleb Bingham, who captured our history on canvas, if you're awed by the accomplishments of George Catlin as he traveled among the tribes of Native Americans and painted them one by one, if you've wished you could see a painting by one of the famous Peale family of nineteenth-century artists (portrait painter Sarah Peale, in this case, who supported herself for many years here in the past century), you won't want to miss this place. Admission is free.

This is the oldest circulating library west of the Mississippi, and in addition to art, you can find rare books: Americana, westward expansion, river transportation, etc.

Or how about a museum of money? Nearby at Seventh and Washington, you'll find the **Mercantile Money Museum.** Visit daily from 9:00 A.M. to 4:00 P.M. and see rare coins and currency; admission, ironically, is free.

While you're in the neighborhood (maybe you went to Busch Stadium?), stop in at the **National Bowling Hall of Fame and Museum** at Eighth and Walnut; Ralph Kramden woulda loved it. If you picture bowling as a recent invention, something you do on a Saturday night with a couple of cold brewskis, think again; it dates back to ancient Egypt. The history of the game is traced in 50,000 square feet of exhibits that include everything from visitor-activated computers to functioning antique lanes.

This is certainly the area for history buffs. Just a couple of blocks west of the Arch and Laclede's Landing is the Old Courthouse, now yet another wonderful museum. Permanent displays include exhibit rooms featuring the early years from 1764 to 1850, the growth years from 1850 to 1900, early twentieth-century displays from 1900 to 1930 and from that date to the present, plus dioramas on the westward expansion originally designed by Works Progress Administration (WPA) artists during the Great Depression.

If the Arch's view is too modern (or too frighteningly high) for you, book a tour to the top of the courthouse dome by calling (314) 425–6017. *This* vantage point has been here for 125 years— well worth the effort.

Grant's Farm, 10501 Gravois Road (314–843–1700), is a Clydesdale breeding farm so named because General Ulysses S. Grant once farmed part of its grounds. August Busch, Jr., of Anheuser-Busch beer fame, owns the 281-acre estate, but you can tour the grounds on a trackless train, see the collection of Clydesdale-drawn carriages, or admire the log home built in 1856 by General Grant himself.

If you are in the city, look for **Miss Hulling's Cafeteria** at 1103 Locust Street (314–436–0840). Open Monday through Saturday from 6:00 A.M. to 8:00 P.M., it's a relatively inexpensive spot for "grazing." Lunch averages $5.00 to $6.00 and dinner $7.00 or $8.00. Opened in 1926 with Miss Florence Hulling's life savings of $600, it is run today by her son Steve Apted, who continues to abide by his mom's recipe for success. It has a nostalgic tearoom look with pink latticework and burgundy carpets. Miss Hulling's Cafeteria is the best known of the five eateries in the complex, and features an adjacent bakery and ice-cream shop, freshly ground gourmet coffee, homemade ice cream (try frozen honey custard), and pastries made from scratch.

Fans of ragtime piano won't want to miss the **Scott Joplin House State Historic Site** at 2658 Delmar. The legendary "King of Ragtime" composed some of his best work while living in a small flat at this location; there's a room for musical performances, a tiny sales shop, and exhibit galleries devoted to Joplin's life as well as black history and culture.

A couple of art galleries in the area may pique your fancy— though there are a number of fine galleries to explore in the St. Louis area. Don't let this small sampling give you the idea that's all there is. The **River Road Gallery** in the Swiss Village Bookstore specializes in historical and river art, and it just seems to fit the Old St. Louis feeling around here. It's located in Laclede's Landing at 707 North First Street, and it's open Monday through Friday from 10:00 A.M. to 5:00 P.M., Saturday from 10:00 A.M. to 8:00 P.M., and Sunday from 11:00 A.M. to 5:00 P.M.

The **Austral Gallery** at 2115 Park (314–776–0300) offers original contemporary Australian paintings and drawings, as well as prints and a nice selection of aboriginal art. Hours are Wednesday and Saturday, 1:00–5:00 P.M., or by appointment.

Florissant, just north of downtown St. Louis, is so called because the first inhabitants found it a beautiful, flowering valley. It still is—but that's not all the town has to offer. Jesuit father Pierre Jean DeSmet, champion of the Indian nations, founded the **Old St. Ferdinand's Shrine.** It's now open to the public at 1, rue St. François (314–837–2110). The picturesque St. Stanislaus Jesuit Museum, once a self-sufficient monastery, complements the shrine; it also boasts a surprising collection of rare Greek and Latin tomes dating from 1521. The address is 700 Howdershell Road, just north of Interstate 270. Call (314) 837-3525.

If you prefer to head south instead, you'll find St. Louis's own French Quarter in historic Soulard, 2 miles south of the Arch on Broadway. There's a dandy mix of period architecture and pubs, cafes, and shops for you to browse.

If you want to stay in the St. Louis area, but not in the city itself, there is a cluster of suburban cities nearby. Many of them have bed and breakfast inns available through the **River Country Bed and Breakfast Service** at (314) 771–1993. River Country lists B&Bs throughout Missouri that can be reached only through the service. Ask for Mike Warner; she will have all the information you need, including listings in Des Peres, Ladue, and Creve Coeur.

Okay, it's easy to make jokes about a Dog Museum, and everyone who writes for a living has given it a doggone good try. But man's best friend deserves to be celebrated, and this canine tribute located in the 1853 Greek Revival Jarville House in St. Louis County's Queeny Park, about 18 miles west of the St. Louis riverfront, is a gallery worth a visit if you are seeking the best art of dogdom. Begin with the oil-on-mahogany portrait of the ex-Presidential pet Millie, the English springer spaniel who called the White House home for four years. See a sculpted bronze whippet, a massive wooden mastiff (once part of a carousel ride), and many works of art commissioned by breeders of show-winning dogs. Coonhounds, retrievers, and herders join dalmations, bloodhounds, and Afghans. Pekingese, wolfhounds, and dogs of every variety, including those of more mixed heritage, are celebrated in paintings, woodcarvings, ceramic figurines, and photographs that show them doing what dogs do—sniffing, running, licking, sleeping, or just being there. The gift shop will give you paws for thought with posters, stationery, and dozens of trinkets bearing likenesses of dogs and dog accessories (tie clasps made of tiny dog biscuits, for example).

Every Sunday afternoon the popular "Dog of the Week" program features a guest breeder, trainer, or veterinarian and a dog for demonstration. A book and videotape library allows potential dog owners to judge the merits of various breeds. In the past, well-mannered dogs were welcome to tour the gallery with their owners, but because of too many "accidents," that was stopped. The Dog Museum at 1721 South Mason Road is open from 9:00 A.M. until 5:00 P.M. Tuesday through Saturday and from noon to 5:00 P.M. on Sunday. Take I-64/Highway 40 west past the I-270 loop, exit on Mason Road and drive south. Watch for the signs. Admission is $3.00 for adults, $1.50 for ages 60 and up, $1.00 for children ages 5 to 14. The Dog of the Week program begins around 2:00 P.M. Call (314) 821–DOGS for more information.

Wine Country

Outside St. Louis on Interstate 44 West (which, by the way, follows old Route 66 from "St. Louie to Joplin, Missouri . . .") is the town of ↄ**Eureka,** which houses sixty-four antiques and craft shops. Pick up a complete list of shops at the first one you spot as you come off of the interstate. This town could be a one-stop, shop-till-you-drop experience, but that would be crazy, because you are now heading into an antiques-hunter's heaven.

Between Eureka and the town of Pacific is a place to slow down, be quiet, and meditate. The **Black Madonna of Czestochowa Shrine and Grottos,** operated by the Franciscan Missionary Brothers, is located here. Whether your interest is historical or spiritual, don't miss this one. Take a guided tour or just have lunch in the large picnic pavilion. Call (314) 938–5361.

Midwesterners seem to have a deeply rooted preference for smoked flavor, probably from all those nights our ancestors spent around a campfire; who can resist a terrific country ham, hickory-smoked bacon, or a tender slab of ribs? You won't have to if you pay a visit to the **Smoke House Market** at 16806 Chesterfield

Airport Road in Chesterfield (314–532–3314). Everything is smoked the natural way, with no preservatives and real hickory smoke. Smoked pork chops, lamb chops, Cajun sausage, along with the ribs and bacon, are available in the shop. Check out the grocery section, as well—some of the top names are represented here. Doesn't maple sugar beans sound irresistible? Owners Thom and Jane Sehnert planned it that way, and Jane's got the background for it; her folks had owned the business since 1952.

The Sehnerts branched out recently and opened **Annie Gunn's** next door, a grill with an Irish theme, complete with Irish potato soup and a menu of unusual sandwiches and meat from the smokehouse. The most popular is the boursin burger covered with highly spiced garlic and herb cheese. And there is the braunschweiger sandwich, the Cajun sausage sandwich, fabulous smoked lamb chops, ribs, Reubens, French dips . . . and the list goes on.

To find the smokehouse, follow your nose, or if your sniffer isn't highly trained, follow Highway 40 to the Airport Road exit and double back; it's about 30 miles west of St. Louis.

Highway 100 along the Missouri River is a beautiful drive any time of the year because of the white sycamores marking the river's course; in autumn it's spectacular. The Missouri River Valley deserves plenty of time; there's a lot to see and experience.

St. Albans is an anachronism, a tiny, planned community founded in the 1930s by the Johnson Shoe Company family. Five thousand acres of gorgeous rolling hills and meadows reminded Mr. Johnson of an area in England known as St. Albans, and he made it into a working farm. It is some 30 miles west of the city limits of St. Louis on Highway 100, a dandy day trip and a destination not to be missed.

Aficionados of French cuisine may remember Le Bistro in the town of Chesterfield. Restaurateurs Gilbert and Simone Andujar closed that place when highway work made it difficult to get to, but take heart. Simone spotted the lovely gardens of St. Albans and chose the location for a new restaurant, **Malmaison** (314–458–0131). (Those whose French is a bit tenuous may wonder if the name means "bad house," and it would if it were two words. Native Frenchwoman Simone says that the lovely flowers reminded her of the garden where Josephine met Napoleon in her homeland, a garden named Malmaison.) The dining experience here is superb, as is the food; it's a favorite retreat for St.

Louisians. Hours are Wednesday through Sunday, 11:30 A.M. to 2:30 P.M. for lunch and 5:00 P.M. to 9:30 P.M. for dinner (10:00 P.M. on Saturday).

Hard-core bicyclists love the St. Albans region for the challenging hills near the Missouri River and the great views. They never miss the little country store here, **Head's Store,** run by Mae Head; she's a pistol. Usually, the bike riders have just come from the smokehouse at Chesterfield. All that expending of energy requires fuel and plenty of it!

⊃**Hunter's Hollow Inn and Restaurant** (314–742–2279) in Labadie at Washington and Front streets is a wonderful side trip for a country lunch or dinner—or a bit of relaxation at the Decoy Lounge. Take your pick: The dining room offers classic French country cuisine by chef Claude Courtoisier or Missouri hickory-smoked specialties. B&B facilities are also available.

This is Missouri's Rhineland, the wine-growing region. Both oenophiles (wine connoisseurs) and devotees of wine coolers will enjoy tasting what the state has to offer. There are two schools of thought about Missouri wines: Some say that because a majority of the grapes grown here are European vines on wild grape or Concord root stock (and some self-rooted French hybrids), the wines will be different from California or French wines. Others, purists to be sure (and the Mt. Pleasant Winery falls into this category), say that they will hold Missouri's best wines against California wines in a blind tasting any day and challenge connoisseurs to single them out. They have done so for Les Amis du Vin, or Friends of Wine—a wine-tasting club. Whether you are a member of Les Amis du Vin or just a wine lover, you will notice that the wines of Missouri are as varied as the vintners who make them, so don't judge Missouri wines by the first place you stop.

The Frene Creek white wines rival those of the Rhine River Valley. Pop wine drinkers will love Missouri's blends of fruit wines. The peach wine made by Stone Hill and the cherry wine by Hermanhoff are a treat over ice in the hot summer months.

Washington Landing was first settled in the early 1800s. Lewis and Clark passed through the site of the future town of Washington in search of the Northwest Passage, and pronounced it promising because of its excellent boat-landing site. Located in the curve where the great river reaches the most southern point in its course, Washington is still a good place to stop when headed west.

Willkommen

Missouri River, Hermann

FRESH FISH

Old Waterworks Building, Washington

Washington Station Caboose

Hermann Fest Halle

Attractions in Washington and Hermann

Remember the photos of no-nonsense General Douglas MacArthur with his teeth clamped onto the stem of a corncob pipe? That was a Missouri Meerschaum he was smoking, manufactured right here in Washington. Henry Tibbe invented the corncob pipe, a triumph of ingenuity—and availability—over credulity. Times must have been hard, but corncobs, at least, were plentiful. In days past there were three pipe factories in town, and a number of other little outfits sprinkled around the state; now only the Missouri Meerschaum Factory and the Buescher Factory—both in Washington—crank out the plaster-lined pipes. You can learn all about it at the **Washington Historical Society Museum** at Main and Cedar streets, Saturdays and Sundays from 1:00 to 4:00 P.M.; during the week call (314) 239–2715 to arrange a tour. The Washington Chamber of Commerce is housed here as well; someone will be able to point you in the right direction.

The old 1888 waterworks building on Lafayette Street, down on the riverbank across the railroad track, now houses the ⊃**Progue Sculpture Studio and Bed and Breakfast.** Artist Larry Progue, chairman of the Art Department at East Central College in Union, shows modern sculpture in stainless steel, aluminum, brass, and tin. Larry describes himself as an "abstract expressionist direct metal sculptor." In addition to his sculpture, the stained-glass works of Randy Carter and the work of other artists are also displayed in the gallery.

The living quarters in the building overlooking the river have been restored as a bed and breakfast. The apartment contains two private bedrooms, a sunken bathroom, a kitchen, and a sitting room with such touches as ornate stained-glass ceiling fans. A romantic night on the riverbank includes a bottle of Missouri wine with cheese and crackers and soft drinks. In the morning you can stroll down the quaint riverfront to a cafe for a complimentary breakfast. Rates are $95 per couple ($135 for two couples), with special weekend rates. Call Larry at (314) 239–0668 or –7289.

Speaking of artists, don't miss the **Gary R. Lucy Gallery** at Main and Elm streets. You may recognize Gary's work if you've picked up a Southwestern Bell telephone book from recent years; his work has graced the cover.

Gary is an extremely thorough young man. In order to get just the right feeling in his series of Missouri River paintings, the artist took his boat as far upriver as was navigable, to Ft. Benton, Montana, and explored interesting areas from there back to Washington. No wonder his paintings ring true.

The gallery is open seven days a week—someone will be there if Gary is off on a research trip. It's a two-story building containing the artist's studio, which is open to the public on weekends, if you've a yen to see the place where an artist creates. You won't see the artist at work, though—"makes me too nervous," says Gary.

Just across Front Street and down a bit from Progue's at Lafayette is **Linen & Lace.** This shop, full of lovely European-style lace curtains, bedcovers, and tablecloths, occupies a Federal-style building beside the river. Owner Sunny Drewell's business has done so well that she closed the Zechariah Foss Bed and Breakfast upstairs and moved Linen & Lace into the entire building. Their mail-order catalog is a charmer, photographed right here in the house. If you can't make it to Washington (much less to Europe) in person, call (800) 332–LACE to get the Linen & Lace catalog.

Right across the street you can spend a night steeped in history. The 1837 **Washington House Inn** first served as an inn; it has since put in its time as a general store, riverboat captain's house, fish market, speakeasy, restaurant, and apartment house. Now it has come full circle, offering nineteenth-century lodging combined with contemporary comforts. All rooms feature views of the Missouri River, queen-size canopy beds, private baths, and complimentary wine and cheese, and the inn serves breakfast. Stenciled walls and period furniture, mostly from the Missouri Valley area, add to the ambience. Take time to unwind and watch the river traffic and trains from the balcony or terrace. (If you find the sound of night trains romantic, the tracks are just across the street.)

Reservations are $65 per night (314–239–2417); smoking is prohibited due to the historic nature of the building and its furnishings. Downstairs is a tiny shop called **. . . not just Cut and Dried,** owned by Carolyn McGettigan, who has a wonderful selection of coffees, herbs, teas, and dried bouquets. Sit down and have a steaming cup of cinnamon coffee with Carolyn and she will make scouting Washington easier (314–239–9084).

Stroll on down to 116 West Front Street and have lunch at **Lucinda's.** This little bistro has the kind of food men seem to love, for example, the roast beef croissant with grilled onions and mozzarella cheese. And chef Joan Maune can turn out desserts that are just plain irresistible to them. Reading the menu offers more temptation than most people can stand—things like Kentucky Bourbon Pie and the best cheesecake anywhere. But the little touches make the cafe memorable for women as well. Fresh flowers on each table and individual salt cellars and spoons add a touch of elegance to the antiques-filled room. An antiques shop is also there for browsing. Hours are from 10:00 A.M. until 4:00 P.M. every day but Monday. Lunch is served from 11:00 A.M. until 2:00 P.M. weekdays and until 3:00 P.M. on weekends. Owner Walt Larson lives in historical figure Lucinda Owen's 1838 home in Washington and has plans to open it as a bed and breakfast soon, so you might check with him if you plan to stay in the area. Call (314) 239–9449 for more information.

Only fifty years or so after Meriwether Lewis, his dog Scannon, and his partner William Clark passed by this likely town site, Bernard Weise built his home and tobacco store here on Front Street.

Now that location holds **Lehmann's,** and although the magnificent view is still one of soft moonlight reflecting on the river flowing outside, inside white tablecloths await lovers of fine food and wine. Max and Sandy Lehmann serve food so good you may never want to leave but simply eat your way through the moderately priced menu. Max is a European-trained chef who specializes in German food—Weinerschnitzel, sauerbraten, and the like. Sandy creates luncheon salads for every taste. A real show-stopper is the Riverboat Salad, a halved pineapple filled with fresh seasonal fruit. Homemade bread and rolls round out the reasons for dining here, and the wine list includes wines from Missouri, California, and France.

Of course, the desserts are always a good reason, among gourmet sweet-tooths, to choose a place to dine. Here Max excels with his whimsical creations that are different every night. A favorite is his homemade white chocolate ice cream, perhaps with some of his incredible chocolate cake. And his white chocolate cheescake sells to most people (who don't think they want dessert) when the waiter describes it.

From Wednesday through Saturday, hours for lunch and dinner begin at 11:00 A.M. and end when everyone is gone, about 9:00 P.M. on weeknights, later on weekends. Sunday brunch is just too good to be true for $6.25. An array of food that will compete with any fine hotel in any big city is served after church from 11:00 A.M. until 2:00 P.M.

Some Sunday evenings are set aside for a gourmet wine dinner for those lucky enough to sign up. These special evenings include a seven-course meal and five wines. The cost is $70 a couple. Call (314) 239–9912 to get on the mailing list and see what the menu will be for the next one.

On Friday and Saturday nights the **Creamery Hill Cafe** at Fifty and Cedar is the place for fine dining that includes fresh seafood and the best wine list in town. (Local "foodies" consider this home.) Dinner is served from 5:30 P.M. till 9:00 P.M.; the phone is (314) 239–7127.

You are deep into wine country here, and there is no shortage of wineries along the valley. Most offer tastings; you can choose the ones most convenient for your schedule and location. Some offer unusual wines and are well worth the effort to search out.

Continue upriver on Highway 100 to New Haven. Look for the **Augustin River Bluff Farm Guest House.** Filled with family antiques, it's a comfortable retreat perched high on a Missouri River bluff. There's room to stretch out here, room to breathe—you'll find ninety-nine acres for walking or hiking. Watch barges ply the river from the upstairs porch or from his and hers out-door bathtubs (with a glass of wine, why not?), relax in the front porch glider, or have a wine picnic under the splendid sugar maples. In the evening, enjoy the music room with its restored player piano. When you can't stay awake another minute, comfortable queen-size beds await.

The house is a twenties-style farmhouse on land purchased by Louis and Mary Kraft Augustin in 1910. It has been lovingly restored by the Augustins' two grandchildren and their spouses. It's open year round, so when you get the yen to relax, call (314) 239–3452 for directions and reservations. The farm is on a rural route near New Haven. Robert "Buzz" and Mary Lee Kliethermes and Rich and Cindy Luecke are proprietors. Rooms are $100.

One of the newest wineries in the Missouri Valley region, **Röbller Vineyard** is in a quaint country setting featuring a view of the area's rolling hills. Turn south on the quarry road just east of New Haven, turn right at the first gravel road, and proceed ⅛ of a mile to the winery. Phone (314) 237–3986.

The town of New Haven sits quietly on the river, and there are a number of places worth looking for downtown. Carol Hebbler has a shop and bed and breakfast at the **One Twenty-five Front Street Inn,** (314) 237–3534. The first floor holds **Collections Old and New,** a shop filled with flowers, antiques, crafts, and collectibles of all sorts. Above the shop is an apartment filled with fine antiques. A bottle of wine and fresh flowers await guests. The apartment (which will sleep four) has a living room, working kitchen, dining room, and private bath, as well as a bedroom suite with a sitting room where you can curl up in an antique swing and watch the river flow by. The rooms are huge; the bedroom has a queen-size bed, and it is $85 including a continental breakfast in the morning. There is also cable television, a VCR, and a stereo hidden among the antiques.

Just down the street is **Meriwether's** at 130 Front Street, (314) 237–4100. Barbara Spellman-Scott recently moved the restaurant here from Washington. Moving to a new town didn't change the quality of the food, though. She still does all the cooking, and her ever-changing menu is still filled with fresh meat and produce. She continues to offer sinfully rich desserts (Murder by Chocolate is a dense, rich, flourless chocolate cake drizzled with raspberry sauce, chocolate sauce, and of course, whipped cream—earning its name), the same charming ambience, the same trains going by outside. Three different menus for lunch, served from 11:00 A.M. until 2:00 P.M. Tuesday through Saturday; dinner on Thursday, Friday, and Saturday nights at 5:00 P.M. (the kitchen closes about 9:00 P.M.); and Sunday brunch from 11:00 A.M. till 3:00 P.M. make it likely you will eat here several times. Dinner on Saturday night features live piano music. The dress is what Barbara calls "smart casual." Don't miss this fine restaurant.

⊃**Bias Vineyards & Winery** in picture-postcard Berger (pronounced BER-jer, population 214) lies on Highway B just off Highway 100. The setting sun at Berger reflects on the river and rugged limestone bluffs; it throws long shadows across the tilled bottomland along the river. Follow the signs to a wooded hillside. As you start up the hill, there is a railroad crossing at the foot of the rise to the vineyards, (It could be dangerous when you leave; a mirror hangs in a tree to give drivers a view of the tracks, so proceed slowly.)

Owners are Jim and Norma Bias. Jim was a TWA captain based in St. Louis. They bought the land fifteen years ago when they were looking for a country spot within commuting distance to St. Louis's Lambert Field. It came with seven acres of vines. "We had to do *something* with the grapes," says Norma, so they invested in a roomful of stainless-steel tanks and went into the wine business. One thing led to another, and soon Norma was in the banquet business.

Saturday night buffet dinners are scheduled on the vineyard grounds from April to December; reservations are a must. Gourmet meals are served along with Bias wines. The Biases have recently bought a building in downtown Berger (two doors up from the post office and across from the church) and are in the process of making it into a bed and breakfast (314–834–5475). Winter is less hectic and the Biases invite cross-country skiing on their property when the snow comes. They offer vine cuttings during pruning season (January) for creating wreaths or smoking meats. If it's too far to drive home, Norma suggests the **Tuck Me Inn** at Berger, (314) 834–5554.

Next on the road is Hermann. To orient yourself, begin at the Hermann Visitors' Information Center at 306 Market Street. Jack Haney, the guy with the moustache and Bavarian hat, also runs Whiskey Jack's Museum of Prohibition-era memorabilia. He will tell you all about Hermann. Founded in 1836 by members of the German Settlement Society of Philadelphia, it was intended as a self-supporting refuge for German heritage and traditions, a sort of "second fatherland."

George Bayer, who had immigrated in 1830, selected a site in Missouri that resembled his home in the Rhine Valley in terms of climate, soil, and richness of wild grapevines. Bayer and the other German immigrants dreamed of building one of the largest cities in the United States on the Frene Creek Valley.

The dream quickly attracted a variety of professionals, artisans, and laborers who began the task of building the city of their dreams. It never did become that giant metropolis of the immigrants' dreams; now it is a city of festivals. There is Maifest, Wurstfest, and Octoberfest, each drawing thousands of folks from all over. Amtrak helps to alleviate traffic on festival weekends.

In winter and on non-festival weekends, Hermann is just what it looks like—a quaint German town, quiet, and filled with B&Bs, from the huge White House Hotel to the tiny Seven Sisters Bed and Breakfast Cottage. You'll find galleries, shops, and brick homes snugged right up to the street, European style. During the festivals, though, it becomes crowded and noisy, as busy as Bayer's dream city. Portable toilets appear on street corners, and the revelry spills from wineries downtown. If you want to be off the beaten path around here, you should aim at a weekday in the off-season. Then a traveler has this sleepy hamlet all to himself.

The **Stone Hill Winery** on Stone Hill Highway just off Twelfth Street (314–386–2221) is owned by Jim and Betty Held. The world-renowned cellars are carved into the hillside, and there's a breathtaking view of the town. **Vintage 1847 Restaurant** shares the picturesque hilltop location; a huge window at one end of the restored carriage house looks out on Missouri's blue hills. Visit the restaurant's wine cellar to choose the evening's libation, and do scrutinize the menu carefully—there's a cheesecake to die for. (Take home the *Vintage 1847 Cookbook;* it's a great gift idea.)

Once in town be sure to see the **Hermannhoff Winery Festhalle,** the world's largest wine hall, where you can dance to live German bands every Saturday and Sunday, starting at noon. There is no entrance fee. Enjoy a festival German dinner or a *brat mit krauts* on a bun.

There are so many great little antiques and craft shops that it would be impossible to list them all, but a great bakery is always worth the space. Stop by **LaBoube Bakery** (308 Market) to pick up some homemade baked goods. Many are German specialties; you'll think you're back at *grossmutter's* (that's grandmother's).

There are many B&Bs in Hermann. Among them is ⊃**Birk's Gasthaus,** Elmer and Gloria Birk's place at 700 Goethe Street (314–486–3143). This Victorian mansion was built by the owner of the third-largest winery in the world and is furnished in period antiques, including some 6-foot tubs with gold eagle-claw feet, brass beds, and 10-foot doors with transoms. Birk's offers Mansion Mystery Weekends the first two full weekends of every month. These are sold out months in advance. The Birks write new theme mysteries each month, and the action happens in the gasthaus among the guests, with Showboat Community Theater members as characters—the Halloween mystery stars Frankenstein, for example.

The 12,000-square-foot mansion has twelve bathrooms; some are still being restored. There are nine rooms available now, seven with private baths. Full breakfast includes such delights as sausage casserole, fruit, baked goodies, juice, and coffee. Bed and breakfast rates are $77.50 for a king-size bed and private bath.

Mystery weekends are $200 per person (or share a bath at $175 a person) for two nights, five meals, and two cocktail parties as well as tours of Hermann and the mystery to solve.

Lovers of Christmas—the old-fashioned kind—will love Pelze Nichol Haus Bed and Breakfast, 109 E. Broadway (314–486–3886). The home dates from 1845 to 1850 and is on the Historic Register; it's just across from the Visitors' Center off Market Street. Here Jack and Chris Cady have created a Christmas fantasy that lasts all year round. But this isn't your commercial red-and-green image. It's all natural, old-style German, with subdued colors and plenty of Pelze Nichols to remind you of the past.

Who is Pelze Nichol, you say? The name means Furry Nicolas, the German Santa—or his helper. (Perhaps you recognize him as Belznickle, instead.)

Stay in one of three rooms, the Christmas Room, the Tannenbaum Room, or the Christmas Morning Cottage, each with its own tree made by Chris herself, and each with a private bath. Don't miss the Santa Shop, also on the premises—after spending time in this delightful place, you'll want to take home a Pelze Nichol of your own; Chris makes all style and sizes.

The **Historic Hermann Museum** is in an old schoolroom that still contains the original slate boards and desks. Mildred Pehle, who works at the museum, was once a student here; she says they are "still carrying on the German tradition." Hermann has a student exchange program sister city in Arolson, Germany.

Get off of Highway 100 and go west on Highway C to Bonnots Mill at the confluence of the Osage and Missouri rivers, where Lewis and Clark camped and the first and oldest French trading post in the country was built. You will drive down from the high hill where you can see forever.

Find Ɔ**Krautman's Korner Cafe** (314) 897–4346 for some great food at reasonable prices. Cliff and Billie Mantle serve steaks, prime rib, fried chicken, Cajun catfish, and hot spiced shrimp. There is a bar and a wine list and even an 800 number, which belies the name cafe and shows it for the full-line restaurant it really is. Call (800) 769–7358 or (314) 897–4346. Hours are from 11:30 A.M. to 9:30 P.M. Thursday through Sunday.

The tiny town of Bonnots Mill itself is picturesque. Jefferson City's active sketch club has come here to work; the views of the autumn foliage and the silvery river are glorious—you may find yourself in a work of art.

The small village of Westphalia, south on Highway 63, perches like a lighthouse on the hill. There is only one street, with homes built right up to the sidewalk as they are in Hermann. Everything is spic and span and a pleasure to the eye—*das gut.*

The **Westphalia Inn** (314–455–9991) offers family-style meals—mashed potatoes and gravy, green beans, and an unbeatable fried chicken dinner. It is nothing fancy, just good old "comfort food" at reasonable rates. Tom and Melody Buersmeyer feed folks from 5:00 P.M. to 8:00 P.M. Thursday through Saturday and Sunday from noon until 8:00 P.M.

There is also a bed and breakfast in a distinctive home that connects to the post office, with a private suite and plenty of room for extra guests. Rates are $45 to $50; make reservations through the **River Country Bed and Breakfast** (314–965–4328).

Farther south on Highway 63, along the Gasconade River, lies Freeburg, a great spot for a float trip on the river; there are plenty of opportunities to get wet. The access point for the area is the Rock Island Landing, where the Rock Island Railroad crosses the Gasconade River. This trestle bridge was built in 1900—but don't worry, it still carries traffic.

On the east side of Highway 63 at Vienna, the ⊃**Americana Antique, Art and Curio Shop** is a house and garage and several outbuildings (including a huge barn), all filled to the ceiling with what owner John Viessman calls "stuff." Everything you can imagine, from old army uniforms to a disassembled log cabin he is rebuilding—to hold some more stuff. Stuff like time-card racks out of an old factory, pictures, ancient trunks, and dolls. Not just little stuff, but *big* stuff, like a walnut wardrobe that measures 6 feet wide and 9 feet tall. But his real passion is books, especially books about Missouri history, and there are over 30,000 books in the house, two deep in floor-to-ceiling shelves running through what was once the living room. Volumes on the Civil War, Jewish folklore, and the black experience in America are crammed together in some kind of order ("it's a constant struggle," he says) along with old Dick and Jane books and McGuffy Readers and an 1824 textbook. Books are everywhere among the other stuff, too. There is a whole wall of *Life* magazines set up by year so that people can find their birthday issue. John still goes to auctions and sales and carts more stuff home, and he has been doing this for over twenty years. He and his wife Kelley McCall have a studio there, too—Kelley is a photographer, and John paints. He is around most weekends, when he isn't at a sale, and the shop is open by chance or by appointment. There's a large sign in the front yard announcing OPEN or CLOSED so you can just drive by and check it out (314–422–3505).

Vienna has only about 600 residents, but what an interesting bunch of folks they are! While in town you can visit weavers Jim and Sherry Bingham, or visit Tom Coffey's **Swap Shop** (314–422–3314) and let Tom talk your ear off. There are two craft shops in town, an antiques shop, an art collection in the courthouse, a mural depicting the one-room schoolhouses in the school cafeteria (painted by John Viessman), and the Langebert Hat Company, specializing in rabbit-fur hats (314–422–3377). There's even a recording studio in town that people from Nashville come up to use. The Old Jail Museum is 3 blocks east on Highway 42, and you can visit it from 2:00 P.M. until 4:00 P.M. on Sunday in the summertime. Two miles down the Ball Park Road is one of nine swinging bridges left in the state. The circa 1855 Latham Log House has been restored in the community park, also on Ball Park Road.

The community of Pay Down, 10 miles east of Vienna on Highway 42, is a ghost town now. A large grist mill, old Pay Down Store and post office, and the old Bray mansion still stand. All are privately owned.

Next up on Highway 63 is Rolla. Here the famous **Rolla School of Mines** is located. If you are interested in mines or minerals, it's worth your while to see the museum. (Don't miss Rolla's "Stonehenge.")

There are plenty of antique shops in the area, but a special place is George Carney's **Memoryville, USA** at 1008 West Twelfth Street (314–364–1810). It's a bit-of-everything museum that includes an early twentieth-century town, over sixty antique cars, and an art gallery.

There's a lot happening in St. James on Highway 68 east of Rolla, if you are an oenophile (that's a wine lover, remember?). Stop by **St. James Winery,** at 540 Sidney Street (314–265–7912) or visit ⊃**Heinrichshaus Vineyards and Winery,** a family-owned winery specializing in dry wines, including vidal blanc and chambourçin. Heinrich and Lois Grohe are the owners and wine masters. Heinrich is from southern Germany, and their daughter Peggy went to school in Switzerland, where she studied wine making. The winery offers fresh grapes in season, Missouri cheeses and sausages, hand-thrown pottery, and original watercolors and prints by Missouri artists. Now this is a full-service winery—wine and cheese, a clay carafe, and original art to enjoy while you picnic on the winery grounds. Spring and fall bring festivals and bike tours to the winery. Call (314) 265–5000 for a calendar of events and directions or watch for signs; this is on a rural route. A loaf of bread, a jug of wine, and a picnic!

Deep underground in the unchanging atmosphere beloved to spelunkers, the longest underground river flows silently through Ɔ**Onondaga Cave** in the Daniel Boone State Park near Leasburg on Interstate 44 east of St. James. This is a place of superlatives: Massive stalagmites rise like peaks from the floor of the Big Room, the largest living cave room in the world. In Daniel Boone's Room the abundance of cave formations is enough to make you shake your head in amazement. Old Dan himself discovered the place in 1798—or rather, he was the first white man to do so. Native Americans had used the area as a hunting sanctuary from earliest times.

Organizers of the St. Louis World's Fair in 1904 encouraged the cave's owners to open it to the public—it was a great hit, as visitors came first by railroad and then by surrey and wagon to explore the wonders.

Bourbon, off of Interstate 44, was once a whiskey stop on the railroad—could you tell from the name? Now it's the home of **Meramec Farm Stays,** modeled after the Australian incarnation of the bed and breakfast experience. Into its fifth generation, this family farm has earned the Missouri Century Farm sign awarded by the University of Missouri to farms that have been in the same family for at least one hundred years.

This is a real working farm, with critters and all—kids who don't have a grandma in the country will enjoy petting the horses, feeding the ducks, or playing in a real old-fashioned hayloft.

It's great for adults, too. If you want to help out around the farm, you may. If not, just enjoy the 1½-mile trail that adjoins the highest bluffs on the Meramec River. Take a dip in a swimming hole, picnic on a gravel bar, or enjoy canoeing on a section of the Meramec that doesn't require a class-five rapids expert.

Rates are $30 to $60; there's a price break for two nights. Children under twelve are $15 a night. Carol Springer asks that you call ahead (314–732–4765) for reservations and directions. It is a working farm, and drop-ins tend to arrive at just the wrong time; but Carol and her husband David Curtis have been juggling it all for eleven years now, so they must be doing something right.

⊃**Meramec State Park Lodge** at Sullivan, east on I–44, is an excellent spot for canoeing and exploring, though it is often crowded on summer weekends. Meramec State Park on the scenic Meramec River winds through the rough, timbered hills just east of little Bourbon.

Missouri is known as the cave state, with more known caves than any other state—5,200 counted so far. There are some twenty-two within the park. One, Fisher Cave, is open for guided tours; others are protected as habitat for an endangered bat species. (You didn't really want to go in that badly, did you?)

The folks at Stanton, farther east on Interstate 44, argue with the people of St. Joseph, who say Jesse James died there. Stanton proponents believe that the murder of Thomas Howard on April 3, 1882, was a clever plot to deceive investigators and authorities— with the backing of then Governor of Missouri, Thomas T. Crittendon! The ⊃**Jesse James Wax Museum** tells the story of James's life in 1882, the mechanics of his incredible escape from justice, and the look-alike outlaw killed by Robert Ford.

Skeptical? Well, that's the true Show-Me attitude. Take your pick: Believe that Jesse died in 1951, just three weeks shy of his 104th birthday, or that he was gunned down by his cousin over a hundred years ago.

Jesse was a member of Quantrill's Guerrillas, who captured a gunpowder mill and used the caverns as hideouts; beneath Stanton's rolling hills lies a complex of caves and finely colored mineral formations, as rare as they are beautiful. The nearby Meramec Caverns have guided tours, restaurants, and lodging.

This area is alive with natural beauty. If you want to stop and get involved, there are plenty of places to camp and canoe. Check out the **Blue Springs Campground and Canoe Rental** at (314) 732–5200; ask for Paul, who will arrange a Meramec float trip or horseback excursion.

Wild Lands

South from St. Louis you have the choice of Interstate 55 or old Highway 61. (You can also take Interstate 270 if you want to bypass the city entirely.) However you get there, don't miss the museum and displays at つ**Mastodon State Park** near Imperial; the kids will love it and so will you.

Did you know that woolly mammoths and mastodons roamed these Missouri hills just a few short millennia ago? This area contained mineral springs, which made for swampy conditions (unfortunately for the mastodons). Large mammals became trapped in the mineral-rich mud, which preserved their remains perfectly as it hardened to stone. You can still see the Kimmswick Bone Bed (one of the most extensive Pleistocene beds in the country and of worldwide interest to archaeologists and paleontologists), or explore the Visitors' Center, with its life-size replica of a mastodon skeleton, clovis points, and other remnants of early human occupation. Mastodon State Park (314–464–2976) is south on Highway 55 at 1551 Seckman Road, Imperial.

Now aim just south for the town of Kimmswick, laid out in 1859 by a German named Theodore Kimm. (We all secretly want to name our own town, right?)

In the early 1880s, Kimmswick's beautiful Montesano Park attracted people from St. Louis by excursion boat. Riverboats and railroads stopped here. But the horseless carriage changed the destiny of Kimmswick; the new highway system bypassed the town, leaving it a sleepy little backwater. Even the trains and boats no longer stopped to trade. But that isn't true any more. Now the *Huck Finn* riverboat paddles down from St. Louis on the second and fourth Wednesday from May through October and docks in Kimmswick; the train may even return soon, but the town no longer worries about being overpowered by St. Louis. Its shops and restaurants are some of the best along the riverfront. The **Christmas Shop** alone is worth diverting from the interstate to see. It is a year-round wonderland guaranteed to put you in the Christmas spirit in the July sunshine.

Mary Hostetter, owner of the つ**Blue Owl Restaurant and Bakery,** says that Kimmswick refuses to be "gobbled up by St. Louis" and works to maintain its individuality as the "town that time forgot." Mary will welcome you personally to sit in front of a cheery fireplace and try a few of her specialties.

The building was erected in 1900 and called Ma Green's Tavern until the fifties. It was restored in the seventies and now has warm wood floors that are charmingly out of level and lace curtains in the windows. Car siding covers the walls, and waitresses in long pinafores serve lunch on delicate blue and white china.

The Blue Owl (314–464–3128) is open year round Tuesday through Friday 10:00 A.M. to 3:00 P.M. and Saturday and Sunday from 10:00 A.M. to 5:00 P.M. From country breakfasts and homemade soups (the Canadian cheese soup is marvelous) on weekdays to the wonderful Sunday special of homemade chicken and dumplings, Mary will try to fill you up. If you happen to see the pastry case as you come in the door, you won't allow that to happen until coffee and dessert. There is outdoor dining May through October and a live German band.

Walk around Kimmswick; there is a lot to see here, from historic homes and businesses to some fine little restaurants, twenty-two shops, so far, and still growing. And do stop by **Kimmswick Pottery.** Artist Chris Ferbet creates hand-thrown pieces, some made from native red clay, which she digs herself. She also carries an international assortment of hand-crafted art. You can watch her working at the pottery wheel or browse around the shop.

The **Old House,** built in 1770, now stands at Second and Elm streets. The second story and wing were added in 1831. When you see the size of the house, it's hard to believe that it was moved from the town of Beck in 1973 to save it from demolition. Inside are several rooms, two of which have massive brick fireplaces to warm the traveler and food perfect for the atmosphere.

There is a new bed and breakfast in town, too. Shirley Berving's **Kimmswick Corner Bed and Breakfast** at the corner of Front and Market streets is upstairs over the Kimmswick Corner gift shop. The two newly refurbished rooms, with shared bath, cost $60 a night. Period wallpaper and antique furniture draw you back to the time when the original owners lived above the shop. You can call (314) 467–1028 and make reservations through the shop, or 467–1027 to leave your name on the recording.

Swing southwest on Highway 67 at Crystal City to the city of Bonne Terre, a year-round resort, as interesting in December in the middle of a blizzard as it is in the heat of a hundred-degree summer day. There isn't all that much to see—above ground, that is. But if you choose Mansion Hill as your first stop and meet owners Doug and Cathy Georgan, the town will come alive for you. In this setting it would have to; the mansion occupies the highest point in Bonne Terre, on 132 acres of timber in the Ozark foothills. Each room has its own view of the estate (which has a 45-mile view of the surrounding area). Four huge fireplaces warm the great rooms.

The 1909 mansion was built by the lead-mining baron responsible for ⊃**Bonne Terre Mines** (the world's largest manmade caverns), which honeycomb the earth under the city. Handdug with pick and shovel, the mines are now flooded. They are the pride of the Georgans, who also own West End Diving in St. Louis. The mines can be explored two ways in any weather: by scuba diving, as do hundreds of divers who make the trek to Bonne Terre winter and summer, or by walking the above-water trails.

Your first view of the mine is breathtaking; under the crystal clear water, illuminated from above by electric lights, divers can see all the remnants of the mining days, including ore carts, elevator shafts, buildings—even tools and drills left when the mine was abandoned in 1961. No less a personage than Jacques Cousteau was a guest at the mansion and filmed a dive here.

The Georgans also own the **Bonne Terre Train Depot,** a National Historic Site converted to a saloon and inn. Boxcars and a caboose are parked beside the depot and are being transformed into more B&B suites.

"I needed so much lumber in my restoration projects that we bought a lumber mill just to recreate the original trim and ceiling moldings," says Doug. He and Cathy spent time and money not only in restoration, but also searching out authentic train memorabilia, which includes a nineteenth-century English phone booth and dining and kitchen cars. The north room of the depot is the Whistle Stop Bar. Upstairs are four large suites, all with private bathrooms.

Rates are $100 for two. The mansion and depot are filled almost every weekend, year round, by diving clubs who travel here to scuba dive. All rooms have twin beds to accommodate the divers.

The mining industry has been important to the state since the first inhabitants began to dig red iron oxide for war paint. Early explorers discovered lodes of a "shiny grey mineral" even on the surface of the ground. It was lead, one of the primary ores mined in the state today.

History buffs will enjoy **Missouri Mines State Historic Site** near Flat River just east of Highway 67. The powerhouse of Federal Mill No.3 has been converted into a museum of Missouri mining, history, and technology. Here fluorescent minerals can be viewed under short- and long-wave ultraviolet light. Cut and polished stones, rare fossils, translucent minerals, and jewelry are also on display. The names of small communities nearby, such as Leadington, Mineral Point, and Rivermines, give you some idea why the area was settled.

A detour east on Highway 32 will take you to Hawn State Park near Farmington. Exposures of Lamotte sandstone have eroded to form canyon-rimmed valleys with near-vertical cliffs above sparkling, sandy streams and odd, rounded sandstone knobs that look like overgrown dinner rolls. Because of the sandy bedrock, many of Hawn's 600 species of shrubs, trees, ferns, and flowers can only be found in this area of the state. Its hiking trails and acres of shortleaf pine (Missouri's only native pine), wild azaleas, and ferns make a peaceful and beautiful spot to stop and relax.

History buffs shouldn't miss the Civil War battlefield at **Fort Davidson State Historic Site** at Pilot Knob. You can still see the outlines of the hexagonal fort built in 1863 by Union forces. Flanked on three sides by high hills, the fort was vulnerable to attack from above—which must have been apparent to General Thomas Ewing. After losing seventy-five men in the Battle of Pilot Knob, he had his soldiers muffle their horses' hooves with burlap and evacuate during the night.

If you happen to be on Highway 32 headed westbound for Dillard Mill, canoeing in Salem, or hiking in the Indian Trail State Forest, you might enjoy shopping in Bixby at the ⊃**Good Ole Days Country Store.** You will notice the bright red 1946 Missouri Pacific caboose tucked against one side of the store. Owners George and Charlene Civey have modern gas pumps and Model-A vintage pumps (also painted bright red) out front, and inside is the same blend of old and new. Twenty-five cents buys a cup of coffee (on the honor system) while above your head three O-scale model trains run on a track suspended from the ceiling, complete with flashing lights and whistles. There's more to see. Antiques fill almost every available inch of space on the hardwood floors. Out back is an old log cabin turned antiques store, which also houses a collection of minerals from surrounding hills.

Bixby's general store has never closed since it was first opened in 1906 when the railroad put a siding right next to the store. The store sold everything from casket materials and plows to groceries; locals didn't have to go anywhere else (not that there was anyplace else to go anyway). The store still has a lot of convenience items and a good deli for lunch and ice cream (get a real malt) to eat in the caboose. The only things you can't get are alcohol and tobacco. George is a minister at the local church and draws the line there, but no one seems to mind.

Lesterville may be on the map (and it is, south of Arcadia and west of Hogan on Highway 49), but it's really not a town anymore. This unincorporated village is a quiet little place nestled in wooded country that is dotted with old farms and barns. But just down the road is the **Yellow Valley Forge,** a combination blacksmith shop and pottery that looks more like a contemporary gallery from downtown St. Louis.

Doug Hendrickson makes elegant ironware and, in fact, does a brisk wholesale business in several states. He welcomes visitors—and spectators!—and will accept a commission if you've something special in mind.

Doug shares the shop with partner Lee Ferber, a talented potter whose Peola Valley Pottery is among the state's best. In addition to the de rigueur mugs and crocks, there are some terrific birdfeeders to add pizazz to winter days. Take the old Peola road at the north end of town (it's the only way you *can* go) for 3 miles. Watch for circular red, green, and white signs. When you cross Yellow Valley Creek, you've found Doug and Lee's place.

Just up the road from the forge is **Wilderness Lodge** (314–637–2295), a great old-fashioned Ozarks experience that includes Black River canoe and inner tube floats and hayrides in its package. The lodge is made of logs, and the cottages are quintessential rounded Ozark-river stone, each with a fireplace.

The nearby ⊃**Johnson Shut-ins** (north of Lesterville on Highway N) will surprise you with their rugged beauty, which is like terrain you'd expect to find in Maine or Colorado. These worn and convoluted forms have a story behind them; would you believe Missouri once had its own Mt. St. Helens? Prehistoric volcanic eruptions spewed tons of magma, towering clouds of ash, and acid debris, flattening vegetation and covering whole areas with newly formed igneous rocks. Some 250 million years passed, and shallow inland seas encroached, covering the already ancient volcanic mountains with layers of sedimentary rock. These layers built up until they were hundreds of feet thick over the course of many millions of years.

There were more violent uplifts across the Ozarks; the seas retreated; and rain, wind, and moving water eroded the softer sedimentary rock layers, cutting the river valley ever deeper. Swirling over and between the buried igneous hills, the river scoured and carved potholes, chutes, and spectacular gorges. It is amazing that something as penetrable as water can cut the hardest stone—here's proof.

The Johnson Shut-ins are pocketed away in the scenic St. François Mountains; when you see them, you will understand the name. You feel isolated, hidden, shut in—but without a trace of claustrophobia. Adding to the unique nature of the area are the drought-adapted plants commonly found in the deserts of the Southwest. Scorpions and the rare eastern collared lizard (which rises to an upright position to run on its hind legs and is a treat to see) also find a home in the glades. (Never put on your boots in the morning without first shaking them out—scorpions love hiding places.)

East of the park, the Taum Sauk section of the Ozark Trail leads to **Mina Sauk Falls** (the tallest falls in Missouri) and Taum Sauk Mountain, the highest point in the state at 1,772 feet above sea level. (Okay, no snickering, this is *not* Colorado.)

North of the Shut-ins, through some of the prettiest hills this side of the Great Smokies, is Dillard and the ⊃**Dillard Mill** State Historic Site. Like a Currier and Ives scene beside its mill run, it is one of the state's best-preserved water-powered gristmills. This picturesque red building sits squarely at the juncture of two of the clearest-flowing Ozark streams, Huzzah and Indian creeks. The original mill machinery is still in operation, grinding away.

When you've finished with industrial history, check out the natural history. Dillard has a 1½-mile hiking trail through oak and hickory forests that ends at a pine-topped plateau.

Backtrack a bit on Highway 49 and turn east on Highway 32 to ⊃**Elephant Rocks State Park** near Graniteville. It is the first park in the state to have a trail designed especially for the visually and physically handicapped. Signs along the trail, written in braille and in regular text, describe the origin of the elephant rocks and guide visitors along a paved 1-mile path.

Elephant Rocks is one of the oddest geological formations you're likely to find in Missouri. Here monolithic boulders stand end-to-end like a train of circus elephants, dwarfing mere mortals who stand beside them. Made of billion-year-old granite, the rocks were formed during the Precambrian era when molten rock forced its way to the surface, pushing the earth's crust aside. The magma cooled and hardened slowly as this area became less volcanically active; it broke in vertical cracks, which weathered and rounded to form the huge "elephants." This weathering eventually breaks even the largest rocks down into pebbles and gravel, but not to worry: More stone elephants are in the making all the time. The pink patriarch of the pachyderm herd is Dumbo, who is 27 feet tall and 35 feet long and weighs in at a sylph-like 680 tons.

Washington State Park is a bit north, between Potosi and DeSoto. Here you will find the oldest kind of graffiti: petroglyphs, or Indian carvings in the dolomite rock that may have religious

Elephant Rocks State Park

or ceremonial significance. As with the phrase "Kilroy was here," the meaning escapes us, but these cryptic markings give us clues to the lives of the people believed to have inhabited the area between A.D. 1000 and A.D. 6000. Anthropologists believe these were Middle Mississippian peoples, related to the builders of the Cahokia Mounds in Illinois as well as the mound builders who inhabited the land that is St. Louis today.

A 1½-mile trail winds through the heavily forested hills in the park and the Opossum Track Trail begins and ends at the dining lodge, which is handy if you've worked up an appetite. This 3-mile loop trail passes by the swimming pool, the campground, and the bluffs that overlook Big River. The Park Concessionaire can make reservations for you at Washington's cabins from Memorial Day to Labor Day (314–438–4106). Breakfast, lunch, and dinner are available at the sturdy stone lodge overlooking Big River, as are groceries and camping supplies.

River Heritage Area

If you didn't head off into the wilderness back on Highway 67 at Crystal City but stayed on Interstate 55 or Highway 61, you will now be entering the River Heritage area. From river bluffs and hills to lowlands, from historic towns to waterways, the River Heritage region boasts enough destinations for several vacations. The French influence is visible everywhere you look in **Ste. Genevieve,** from the name itself to the many buildings *a la Française.*

First, stop by the information center on Third Street. Many of the town's homes date to the 1700s and are open for tours. Start with the Ste. Genevieve Museum and then choose among the homes, churches, shops, and country inns dotting the town.

You can't help but notice the **Old Brick House,** built in 1780, at Third and Market. It's owned by Rosie and Judy Schwartz, sisters who now run the restaurant here. Judy says the favorite entree is liver *knaefly,* a liver dumpling. Before you liver-haters turn up your nose, this German cook urges you to try the dish. It wouldn't be a regularly scheduled favorite if it weren't great, right?

Down the block at 146 South Third Street is the circa-1790 ↄ**Southern Hotel** (314–883–3493). Barbara and Mike Hankins saw the old wreck, which had been abandoned since 1980, and fell in love with it. "It was such a mess," Barbara says just a bit wearily, "that finally everything quit working. We stripped it back to the walls and put in state-of-the-art electrical, plumbing, and furnace fixtures." Barbara insists they made it into an bed and breakfast to justify owning it!

It has been open since 1987 with eight guest rooms, each with its own bath. Rooms are from $65 to $105 and include such wondrous breakfast items as strawberry soup, artichoke heart strata (a layered egg-and-bread dish), croissants, and homemade lemon bread with juice and coffee.

Many visitors to Ste. Genevieve are research scholars and genealogists from all over the world. The records at the library, courthouse, and churches are the oldest in the West. Ste. Genevieve calls itself the oldest town west of the Mississippi (more than one Missouri town makes this claim, though) and says "all history of the West begins here."

The **Steiger Haus Bed and Breakfast** is at 1021 Market Street (314–883–5881). Rob Beckerman, who is an owner and the manager, cooks and serves a full breakfast ("I do almost everything," he says), and apple crepes and cheese omelets are his specialty. This two-story house has an indoor pool, and, if you enjoy mysteries, plans a murder on weekends for you to solve. Guests are always suspects, but three actors play various roles, especially dead bodies; Rob says, "We don't want to murder our guests." Rates are $48 for a room or $58 for a suite or cottage.

The **Felix Valle State Historic Site** is a sturdy, elegant, restored French home in Ste. Genevieve. Built in 1818, it represents a decision to build a life in this new country—and to make it a good life, as well. Drive to the north end of Main Street—it ends at the river—and you can catch a car ferry across the river to the Illinois side, where some interesting historic sites can be found. It runs during daylight hours every fifteen minutes or so.

At Perryville on Highway 61 is the **St. Mary of the Barrens Church,** dating to 1827. The grounds are open to walk through; be sure to visit the church's museums. This is also the National Shrine of Our Lady of the Miraculous Medal.

For more history (and fun), detour east a bit on the Great River Road and watch for Tower Rock jutting up 85 feet out of the Mississippi. Don't miss the little German towns of Altenberg, Whittenberg, and Frohna. If you're ready to eat, ⊃**Tric's Family Restaurant** in Altenberg turns out a plentiful supply of home cooking, German style, and wonderful buffets at 5:00 P.M. five nights a week. Most nights offer changing menus, but Saturday it's $5.95 for sauerbraten or bratwurst, and on Sunday the noon buffet is $4.95, closed on Mondays. Tric's (314–824–5387) is on Highway C, and it is owned by Harlin and Rose Oberndorfer. Rose can direct you to other special spots in Altenburg and Frohna, including Lutheran monuments and Missouri's first Lutheran college. In Frohna, stop in at **Imy's General Merchandise** on Main Street, and Imogene and Jerry Unger can give you some directions to local sites (314–824–8486).

Stay on Highway 61, and the next stop is Jackson; all aboard the old Iron Mountain Railroad. The oldest Protestant church west of the Mississippi, the Old McKendree Chapel (circa 1819), a national Methodist shrine, is here, and so is **Trisha's Bed and Breakfast** at 203 Bellevue. It is the family home of Trisha and Gus Wischmann, and it is known here as "The Mueller Haus." There's a relaxed, congenial atmosphere (with respect for your privacy) and a home-cooked breakfast. A delightful resting spot—what more could you ask for? Call (314) 243–7427.

But the best attraction for you railroad fans is still the Ɔ**Iron Mountain Railway;** it's the only steam-powered tourist railroad line in the region. Sights and sounds will carry you back to the late 1800s and the early twentieth century when this was the preferred method of travel.

The "mother line" of nearly all of the smaller rail lines that eventually became the historic Missouri Pacific, the Iron Mountain Railroad is part of the St. Louis, Iron Mountain, and Southern Railway Company. On Saturdays you can take a round-trip ride on the dinner train for $22, which includes dinner. Other round-trip excursions leave at various times during the day. Adults ride for $8.00; kids are half price, and those under two are free.

Civil War and history buffs, listen up; a Civil War Reenactment Weekend is held here every year. For information call the Iron Mountain Railroad at (314) 243–1688.

Jackson is also the home of the **White House Bed and Breakfast** at 802 East Washington, a 1908 Romanesque home with four spacious bedrooms. Call (314) 243–4329 for information. The **Oliver House,** which is the only home on the National Historic Register, has been restored to show the lifestyle during the period from 1850 to 1900 in minute detail. It is at 224

West Adams Street and offers tours on Sunday from 1:30 until 4:30 P.M. May through December. You can call (314) 243–2215 or –7427 for more information.

Farming didn't used to be all air-conditioned tractors and mass production. It was smaller, slower—more human. The **Milltown Museum,** which houses the largest collection of farm equipment in the state, reflects that history. Antique cars, buggies, and surreys in addition to farm implements are featured here. The museum is open April 1 through October 31 on Saturday from 8:00 A.M. to 5:00 P.M., Sunday noon until 5:00 P.M., and weekdays by appointment. Call (314) 243–2444.

While you're near Jackson, take a side trip to Burfordville on Highway 34 East. The **Bollinger Mill** has been in continuous operation for more than 180 years—these people really kept their noses to the grindstone, didn't they? Located on the Whitewater River, the four-story, stone-and-brick structure shares the setting with the Burfordville Covered Bridge, one of four covered bridges remaining in the state.

Bridge building was begun in 1858 and, like much of Missouri's everyday life, was put on hold by the Civil War. The Burfordville bridge was completed in 1868. It is a 140-foot span of incredibly long yellow poplar timbers, which grow handy to the river. It's another excellent setting for artists and photographers, not to mention history and nostalgia buffs.

The hills surrounding the city of Cape Girardeau hide 1,100 acres known as the **Black Forest.** Within this forest lie the villages of New Hanover and Arnsberg, created by the late Burton Gerhardt. Beginning in the 1950s, he constructed thirty-two 1870-style buildings including saloon, general stores, blacksmith shop, sawmill, railroad depot, firehouse, foundry, and boardwalk and Gasthaus on more than 20 miles of roads and bridges, including one of only five covered bridges left in the state. The new owner of the two hamlets, Greg Macke, now opens them for weddings, retreats, picnics, and other group activities. The Boy Scouts have their annual Camporee here the first weekend of May, which attracts up to 500 Scouts to the hardwood forest.

Several times a year Macke holds festivals in the villages, and craftsmen set up demonstrations of leathersmithing, basket weaving, quilting, and art of many kinds. The most popular is the Octoberfest, which reflects the German heritage of the Black Forest. More are planned all the time, so call Macke at (314)

335–0899 to find out what the latest happening is going to be. To find the Black Forest from Highway 61, turn right on Highway W 2.6 miles, jog across the creek to County Road 621, then turn left. At the bridge, bear right onto County Road 638, then turn left through the brown gate. There is a $1.00 admission charge for folks over twelve years old during the festivals.

You're deep in southern Missouri now, and headed for "the Cape." On Interstate 55, Cape Girardeau is the biggest city in the area, with a population of almost 35,000. Like many cities, it has grown too fast for its britches and spread out around its original waterfront area into massive suburban fast-food strips. But Cape Girardeau has preserved its heritage carefully, and it's a beautiful city in spite of—and in the midst of—phenomenal growth. (This growth is an occasional hazard of college towns; Southeast Missouri State University is here.)

Drive through the city and note the many nineteenth-century buildings. The beautiful Glenn House, circa 1880, is a good example. The old Court of Common Pleas has a lovely hilltop setting, and Cape Rock Park is a reminder of the early trading post that pre-dated the city itself. Civil War fortifications still remain in the area. The convention and tourism bureau is at 601 North Kingshighway; if you plan to spend some time here it may pay to stop.

Although the Cape is modern and expanding too fast, all is not lost. Proceed directly down to Water Street, which, as you may have guessed by the name, is along the mighty Mississippi. Unfortunately, a rather tall, ugly wall has been built to protect the area from flood, so the view lacks something—water, to be exact. There is an opening and a deck you can drive onto to enjoy the sights, though, if you are fond of rivers—and who isn't? There's just something about the power of that big river.

Across from the opening is **Port Cape Girardeau** at 19 North Water Street (314–334–0954). Over 150 years old, this building was General Grant's headquarters during the Civil War. Now it is a good restaurant featuring famous barbecued ribs, smoked turkey, and catfish. A full order of ribs is only $7.65, and the smoked prime rib with salad bar and potatoes is the most expensive item at $10.95. There is carryout barbecue, too.

About a block away is what will probably be your favorite place if you have any Cajun instincts at all. ⊃**Broussard's Cajun Restaurant** even has a test on the back of the menu to see if there is a trace of Cajun blood in your veins. The "How to tell a full-blooded, dipped-in-the-bayou Cajun from someone who just wishes he was" test begins with the question "Did your grandmother regularly eat *couche* for breakfast?" and ends with "If someone stepped on your toe would you yell 'ho yii' instead of 'ouch'?" If any of you good ol' boys are missing home, this is the place for you, at 120 North Main (314–334–7235).

The food here is authentic, fire-breathing Cajun. The menu has a glossary of terms and a key to spicy foods for those of you who don't like surprises. It is an inexpensive, casual place, but take enough money to try the Cajun Combo for $16.95, which includes a little bit of everything: shrimp and crab meat gumbo, creole, red beans and rice with sausage, and crawfish and shrimp *étouffée*. Also, if you have room, the special includes a salad and French bread. Other entrees range from the $4.50 all-you-can-eat red beans and rice with sausage to the fried crawfish tails for $12.95.

The Blue Bayou, located next door to Broussard's, features a four-piece band playing blues and dance music every night. Broussard's motto is *"Laissez Les Bons Temps Rouler!"*—let the good times roll. Hours are Monday through Thursday 10:00 A.M. to 11:00 P.M., Friday and Saturday 10:00 A.M. to 1:30 A.M., and Sunday 4:00 P.M. to 10:00 P.M.

Before leaving the area, follow Route B to County Road 472 to Pinecrest to see **Penzel's Azalea Gardens.** For more than twenty-five years Mr. and Mrs. Carl Penzel have created one of the most beautiful settings around here—almost fifty acres of azaleas and flowering bulbs. A spring day here is filled with a canopy of tall pines and multicolored dogwoods, walking paths where stone benches hide in the shade, and thousands of flowers.

Near Cape Girardeau, grits begin to sneak onto the breakfast menu, and the accent begins to sound slightly more southern than midwestern.

Trail of Tears State Park on Highway 55–177 commemorates a dismal date in the history of the country. In 1830, President Andrew Jackson signed a bill authorizing the removal of the Cherokees who lived in North Carolina, Georgia, and Tennessee to make room for white settlement. While many left voluntarily, thousands refused to leave their ancient homelands; more than 13,000 who resisted were herded into corrals, then set on a forced march 1,200 miles to reservations in the West during the winter of 1838–39. A sad skein of rickety wagons, horsemen, and men, women, and children on foot made the exodus to Oklahoma.

The march took its inevitable toll throughout the bitter winter; one-fourth of the disenfranchised Cherokees died during the endless trek, a route lined with hardship, loss, and death. It became known as the Trail of Tears.

On Highway 61 South, watch the signs for ↄ**Lambert's Cafe** in Sikeston, home of "throwed rolls." Lambert's, at 2515 East Malone (314–471–4261), is a most unusual place. Yes, they do throw rolls at Lambert's.

It all began on a busy day in May 1976 when passing rolls real nice-like got too slow and a customer hollered, "Just throw me the *x*#! thing!" Before you could say "thank you kindly," others cried out for service, and they have been throwing rolls at Lambert's ever since.

The folks here take control of your dinner needs—and control is the right word (got to have it when you're lobbing a long one). Want another roll? Sing out and look alive, because one will come whizzing by. To complement the rolls throwed your way, another ladleful of sorghum (Missouri's answer to Vermont maple syrup) will be slopped onto your roll, which is already dripping butter. This will require a trip to the restroom to unstick your fingers. Lambert's is fun, if you like noise and confusion—and a lot of food and attention from the waiters.

If your plate begins to look empty, someone comes by with a ladle of beans, or fried okra, or applesauce and plops it in the middle of your plate; when you finish dinner, you will be full. Very, very full. Then you will discover that they are famous for the size of their slices of homemade pie and cobbler. The drinks are served in gallon Mason jars and the atmosphere is a madhouse on a good day, but it's a spot you can talk about for years.

Old Mountain Region

Now you have a choice—go south to the bootheel or loop back up toward St. Louie. West on Highway 60 toward Dexter, the flat, Kansas-like real estate will begin to curve again in the distance.

Dexter is just a wide spit in the highway, but a spot with Fiddler's, on Business Highway 60. Rick and Marilyn Williams own **Fiddler's** and catfish is the favorite meal. Of course, if you are lucky enough to be there on a particular Thursday night, you could order all the frog's legs you could eat for $9.95. They are open Tuesday from 11:00 A.M. to 9:00 P.M., Friday and Saturday 11:00 A.M. to 10:00 P.M., and Sunday 11:00 A.M. to 9:00 P.M. Dinner, with fixins, runs $4.25 to $8.95. Call (314) 624–3710.

Maybe you saw geese in the air and heard their wild cries as you ate your frog's legs. A short trip will take you through Puxico to ⊃**Mingo National Wildlife Refuge,** a vital 21,676-acre link in the chain of refuges along the Mississippi flyway.

The hills flatten into wetlands and plant varieties change visibly. Mingo Swamp was formed some 18,000 years ago when the Mississippi abandoned its bed, leaving an oxbow that filled in with dense swamp species. Abundant artifacts point to the area's use by native Americans, drawn here by swamp-loving wildlife. (No artifacts can be removed from Mingo, however—arrowhead hunters, take note.)

The area offers boardwalk nature trails and a chance to see wildlife in its natural habitat. There is a resident waterfowl flock as well as thousands of seasonal migrants, and two active bald eagle nests are located on the refuge. Be sure to stop by the refuge visitors' center before heading into the swamp (especially during the winter months)—not only to let someone know where you are going, but to enjoy the interpretive displays. Call (314) 222–3589.

Together with the adjacent Duck Creek Wildlife Area, a state wildlife management area, this is the largest hardwood swamp remaining in the state. Lake Wappapello is also nearby; watch for signs.

If you don't expect to find a museum of fine art in the Ozarks, you're in for a surprise. The ⊃**Margaret Harwell Art Museum** in Poplar Bluff boasts a growing collection of works by contemporary Missouri artists.

Housed in a beautiful 1883 home, the museum has mounted one-man shows by important artists such as sculptor Ernest Trova, Swedish artist Anders Zorn, and Missouri's own Thomas Hart Benton. Docents conduct regular tours of the exhibit. The museum, at 427 North Main, is closed Monday and Tuesday. Call (314) 686–8002. Hours are 1:00 P.M. to 4:00 P.M.

Near Patterson you'll find Sam A. Baker State Park, one of the oldest in the state park system. The park is tucked into the Ozarks' St. François Mountains, which are among the oldest mountains in the United States. They are characterized by conical, domelike hills more than 900 feet high. (The latest official word about whether the Ozarks are hills or mountains is this: If you're coming from Texas, they're mountains; if you're coming from Colorado, they're hills.) Nearby is Mudlick Mountain Natural Area, a 1,370-acre area of oaks and other Ozark forest species that, because of their elevation, have been subjected to lightning, wind, and ice, resulting in a bizarre array of gargoylelike growth forms. You'll also find igneous bluffs, glades (Missouri's desert), and talus fields, known as "rock glaciers." The vast and primitive solitude is like that experienced by early settlers.

Bootheel Region

South of Sikeston you'll find hills that *really* roll. ⊃**Big Oak Tree State Park** tells the story of the 1811 New Madrid earthquake, which altered the topography of the southeast lowlands. All of the land from Cape Girardeau south to Helena, Arkansas, sank from 10 to 50 feet, flooding most of what is now New Madrid, Pemiscot, and Dunklin counties. Rich Bootheel forests were converted to swampland, providing temporary protection for the giant trees. You may see trees 120 to 130 feet tall. Enjoy a bayou setting for picnics or fishing. Big Oak Tree is east of Highway 61–55 off Highway 102.

Nearby ⊃**Towosahgy State Historic Site** (off Highway 77) is sixty-four acres of prehistory. Archaeologists believe the site was inhabited between a.d. 1000 and a.d. 1400. Although other groups had lived in this area before that time, their societies did not reach such a highly organized level as that of the Indians at Towosahgy. Experts believe their use of the Mississippi for trade and transportation contributed to this advancement. The river was the link between Towosahgy and the ceremonial center near the present site of Cahokia, Illinois.

Cotton fields join wheat fields as you approach ⊃**New Madrid** (that's pronounced MAD-rid, much more midwestern than Spanish) on Interstate 55. The Mississippi River Observation Deck offers a panoramic view of the New Madrid oxbow;

8 miles of river are visible from the top of the most perfect oxbow on the Mississippi.

The oldest city west of the Mississippi (see, there's that claim again) has something for everyone. Begin at 1 Main Street. This building, on the banks of the Mississippi near the new observation deck, was once the First and Last Chance Saloon. There were no roads to New Madrid; all of the traffic came off the mighty river. Here was the first (and last) chance to get a drink back in 1783. It is now the New Madrid Historical Museum. Virginia Howell is the tour guide; she's lived here all her life.

New Madrid looks sleepy, dreaming away beside the river. It looks safe. It looks as if nothing much could happen here—indeed, as if nothing much ever had. If that's what you think when you see the place, you're wrong.

It balances precariously on one of the most active earthquake faults on the continent. In 1811, the balance shifted. The earth shrugged. The mighty Mississippi ran backwards, riverboats broke up and sank at their moorings, homes disintegrated before their owners' horrified eyes. The quake was so violent that it rang church bells in Boston.

All is not peace and quiet, even now. Howell says that there is a measurable tremor on the seismographs almost every day that can be felt by local folks. The Center for Earthquake Studies at Southeast Missouri State University informs us that a major quake is not just possible, but inevitable; stresses within the earth slowly mount until something has to give. When it does, there will be damage over an area more than twenty times that affected by a California quake because of the underlying geologic conditions—the ground will literally liquefy.

Residents have developed a wonderful gallows humor—you'd have to! T-shirts read, with a certain quirky pride, "It's Our Fault" and "Visit New Madrid—while it's still here." So, you want real excitement? Head for New Madrid. (Of course, the authors file a disclaimer here. If there's a quake while you're in town, it's not "our fault.")

While in New Madrid, visit the **Hunter-Dawson Home and Historic Site.** Built in 1859 by William Washington Hunter, this crisp white house with its ornate trim and contrasting shutters recalls a more genteel era. The costumed guides who answer all your questions treat you with that special southern charm and add to the atmosphere. A small admission fee is charged.

Hunter-Dawson Home

As you continue south from Sikeston and New Madrid, the land becomes flat bottomland. Southern-style cotton, soybeans, and peaches are the important crops here. From Kennett and Malden on the west to Hayti and Caruthersville on the east, hospitality is just what you would expect in this area of Southern heritage, and Missouri begins to feel like Dixie. Welcome, y'all.

Off the Beaten Path in Southwest Missouri

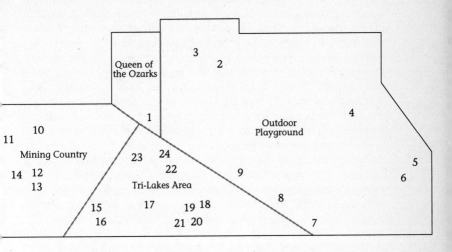

1. Bass Pro Shops Outdoor World
2. The Puzzle Source
3. Big Piney River National Scenic Trail Rides
4. Ozark National Scenic Riverways
5. Jackie's Country Store
6. Big Spring Lodge
7. Grand Gulf State Park
8. Zanoni Mill Inn Bed and Breakfast
9. Laura Ingalls Wilder–Rose Wilder Lane Museum and Home
10. Maple Lane Farm
11. The Gandy Dancer Bar-B-Que
12. George Washington Carver National Monument
13. The Real Hatfield Smokehouse
14. Log Cabin Store
15. Devil's Kitchen Trail
16. Roaring River State Park
17. Omega Pottery Shop
18. Shepherd of the Hills Inspiration Tower
19. Stone Hill Wine Company
20. Hollister
21. School of the Ozarks
22. Cathedral Church of the Prince of Peace
23. Ozark
24. Ye Olde Nixa Mercantile and Sweet Shoppe

Southwest Missouri

Mark Twain National Forests cover thousands of acres of southwest Missouri. Hundreds of miles of hiking and horseback trails free you from even the small, state-maintained highways. If you wander too far off the beaten path here, you will find yourself lost in the woods (and Missouri's bright bluebirds and crimson cardinals will clean up your trail of breadcrumbs).

Many of the lovely, quick-running streams are designated National Scenic Riverways, and the tri-lake area has water, water everywhere. Resort towns are crowded in the summer and deserted in winter. Spring and fall (while school's in session) are just right for exploration. Campgrounds and canoe rentals are everywhere, and there are both gentle rivers for floating and white water for adventure.

If caves are fascinating to you, if you like spectacular rock formations, or if you collect rocks or minerals, southwest Missouri will keep you busy. Truitt's Cave at Lanagan, Ozark Wonder Cave at Noel, the Tiff Mines near Seneca, and the Carthage Marble Quarry at Carthage are a few spots you'll want to check out.

Bed and breakfast fans can write or call Kay Cameron at Ozark Mountain Country Bed and Breakfast Service, Box 295, Branson 65616. Call (417) 334–4720 or (800) 321–8594 for a list of B&Bs in the area. She loves matchmaking and finding just exactly the right place for you.

Queen of the Ozarks

The hub of southwest Missouri is **Springfield** on Interstate 44, the state's third-largest city. Its location on the large grassy uplands of Grand Prairie and Kickapoo Prairie, the rural landscape of the Springfield Plain, is one of the most beautiful in Missouri.

Here's a happy combination of forests, free-running water, and magnificent rock outcrops dotting a farmland that resembles the bluegrass area of Kentucky. Herefords, Black Angus, Charolais, and Simmental graze the cleared uplands. Lespedezas, orchard grass, and fescue glaze the gently rolling pastures with green.

Okay, ⊃**Bass Pro Shops Outdoor World** at 1935 South Campbell—a major intersection in Springfield—is rather on the track. It bills itself as the world's greatest sporting goods store, then lives up to that boast. How many sports shops have a two-story log cabin right in the store? Or a sumptuous restaurant like Hemingway's, serving lobster dinner and a glass of fine wine in front of a room-size aquarium (with white-bellied sharks smiling through the glass and a 15-foot eel hiding in the filter system)?

Across the aerial walkway from Hemingway's is the old-fashioned Tall Tales Barbershop. There is original wildlife art, a museum of the outdoors, trophy animals by the hundreds, and the biggest live bass in captivity. You can buy a hand-knit sweater, get wet beside an indoor waterfall, practice with your new shotgun in the shooting range downstairs, *and* buy a pair of gym shoes or a fishing rod. Just plan on spending a couple of hours when you go in, and take a camera—there are photo opportunities everywhere; you can pose with 10-foot black bears or tiny fawns.

Springfield is a major city, but, as in most big cities, there are hidden treasures. Karol and Nancy Brown's **Walnut Street Inn Bed and Breakfast** at 900 East Walnut (417–864–6346) has a quiet ambience to counter the big-city feel. Each of the eleven rooms includes a private bath, some with original porcelain antique fixtures, hardwood floors, and antique furnishings. Ozark specialties like persimmon muffins and walnut bread are featured along with a full breakfast. Rates are $65 to $120 per night for two persons.

Aesthetic Concerns, Ltd., at 326 Boonville (417–864–4177) is the kind of place that is difficult to find outside a city. It is filled with the things needed to restore an old home or to give character to a new one—fixtures, plumbing, chandeliers, and architectural details. Tom M. Hembree, owner of this collection of unique antiques, keeps hours from 10:00 A.M. to 6:00 P.M. Monday through Saturday.

An outstanding nature center, designed by the Missouri Department of Conservation, is at 4600 South Chrisman (417–882–4237). Want to know how to tell a hawk from a heron when they're far overhead? David Catlin, manager of the center, or one of the volunteers will show you silhouettes suspended from the ceiling that correspond to identifying shapes on the floor. Another room invites you into the dark with displays that light up—or sing out—as you press a button or break a light beam. See a barred owl, hear a whippoorwill, watch a flying squirrel—it's all here. Outdoor nature trails take you through

Ozark woodlands and a small bog; learn while you take in the fresh air.

Springfield is another busy college town, with great places to eat on virtually every corner. Homesick college kids find **Aunt Martha's Pancake House** (417–881–3505) at 1700 East Cherokee, just off Glenstone. Owner Ruth Freeman took over the business from Ozark Opry star Aunt Martha (Willy Nelson washed dishes here for a time), and Ruth continues to coddle customers with from-scratch pancakes and waffles, buttermilk biscuits, and fresh sausage. No chemical aftertaste here! Service is prompt and friendly; lunches and dinners are as hearty and satisfying as breakfast. Try the Po' Boy Sandwich; it's Ruth's answer to the more expensive Reuben, and it's a fine retort.

Springfield is a mecca for watercolorists. For thirty years the **Springfield Art Museum** (417–866–2716) has been the locus for Watercolor USA, one of the most prestigious shows in the nation. Every June and July the museum displays the best and the brightest; you may browse or buy at 1111 Brookside. (You'll know you're close when you see the large yellow sculpture called "Sun Target"; local kids call it "The French Fries.") The museum owns a fine permanent collection of original works. Visit at any time of the year.

Outdoor Playground

Just outside Springfield on Highway 65 is another kind of mecca—tiny Galloway is wall-to-wall antiques. It's as if the town had been invaded by aliens selling oldies; nearly every building and home is now a shop. Find everything from a vine-and-thorn-wrapped birdhouse (to discourage cats, of course) to European china, but don't stop before you get to the flea market a half-mile or so north of the other shops. Here are two floors of great bargain flea market antiques.

Ten miles or so north of Springfield on Highway 65 is the little town of Fair Grove, with its restored buildings full of craftspeople and shops. It's only 3 or 4 blocks off 65; slow down or you'll miss it. Watch for **Mercantile Antiques,** an old storefront building that features antiques as well as pottery and the fine overshot weaving of Marge Wallis, among other things. Through the week, you'll catch the crafters from 10:00 A.M. until 5:00 P.M., but not to worry—if you're passing through on a Sunday after-noon, you'll find them open for business from noon until 5:00 P.M. (417) 759–7794.

Head north on Interstate 44 to Lebanon, a town loaded with surprises. Flea markets and antiques shops are all over the place, more than twenty-three at last count.

Begin at **Rubyette's Floral and Flea Market,** 573 North Jefferson (417–588–2498). Rubyette Bumgardner will gladly chat with you while she works on silk flower arrangements. She knows every place in town and will direct you to other shops with antiques and collectibles, such as Hall-Moore Stuff Company (don't you love that name?), owned by Carol Hall and Ada Moore. Hall-Moore (417–532–3404) is on old Route 66, 1½ miles north of Lebanon—and the list goes on. Pick up a map at Rubyette's. Hours are 9:00 A.M. to 6:00 P.M. Monday through Saturday, 12:30 P.M. to 6:00 P.M. on Sunday.

If you are a dyed-in-the-wool bargain hunter, hit the **VF Factory Outlet** at 2020 Industrial Drive (314–588–4142). You can see it from the Interstate at exit 130, next to the Lee Jeans outlet. It is open 10:00 A.M. to 7:00 P.M. Monday through Saturday. Here are a number of factory outlet shops—Vanity Fair and Lee Jeans included—offering good prices on name brands. With the factory discount, plus a sale, plus a coupon the cashier may give you, you could walk away with a pair of $40 stone-washed jeans for five bucks.

つ**The Puzzle Source** is not for everyone, but if you are a jigsaw puzzle fan, this is a must. Keith and Nancy Ballhagen have the only jigsaw puzzle shop in the Ozarks, with the world's smallest puzzle (2¼ inches by 2½ inches with 99 pieces) and the world's largest puzzle (3½ feet by 9 feet, 7,500 pieces). There are double-sided puzzles, round puzzles, and puzzles within puzzles. Movie poster puzzles, postage stamp puzzles, and puzzles covering any subject you can think of. The most popular is the Route 66 puzzle (600 pieces). Nancy says they just always liked to do puzzles, especially when the children were young, and it sort of grew into a business. Now they have more than 1,200 puzzles displayed in their shop. To find puzzle paradise, take exit 135 (Sleeper exit) from Interstate 44 and follow the east outer road ¾ mile to the first mailbox on your left—you can see it from the freeway. Hours are 8:00 A.M. to 7:00 P.M. during the summer months and 9:00 A.M. to 5:00 P.M. in the winter, or call (417) 286–3837.

Enough shopping—on to serious eating. The **H & J Barbecue** (417–588–1440) on Highway 64 between Bennett Spring and Lebanon is a real family pleaser. The hickory-smoked aroma will lure you inside, but the barbecued ribs and chicken and fat French fries—all fresh and from scratch—will keep you happy here.

Log Cabin Canoe and Outfitters, Chuck and Wanda Robbins's campground (417–532–6439), near Lebanon and Moon Valley, is snugged between the Niangua River and beautiful high bluffs off of Highway 64 east of Lebanon. This campground tries to separate church groups and scouts from "party people" to make happy campers of everyone. Not just a campground and rental place, they offer a package float trip that comes with a cookout breakfast, free showers and firewood, a dinner barbecue, and a hayride for the kids. If you have never been canoeing, southwest Missouri is the place to try it. There is water suitable for beginners as well as white water for the more experienced, year-round floating, and April through October camping.

The Ho-Humm Campsite (for the quiet folks) is 7 miles north of Bennett Spring on County Road 64999 (417–588–1908). The party people prefer Moon Valley south of Bennett Spring on Highway 00 (2 miles on Highway 00, then turn right). Both are riverfront camps. The charge is $2.00 a person ($4.00 if you have your own canoe plus a $2.00 take-out charge for the canoe).

Native Americans who first inhabited the **Bennett Spring State Park** area referred to the beautiful blue spring as "the eye of the earth." Early settlers found the spring, which pumps an average of one hundred million gallons of water a day, an ideal location for grist and flour mills. The last mill was destroyed by fire in 1944, but today trout fishing flourishes. (On opening day, anglers are elbow to elbow, but they still manage that elegant dry-fly cast.)

The Nature Interpretive Center (417–532–3925) is open daily during the summer and Wednesday through Sunday from September through May. A full-time park naturalist provides guided nature walks. Camping is available, or rent a rustic, romantic cabin with a fireplace for $45.

A small side trip north on Interstate 44 will quickly take you to Waynesville and the ⊃**Big Piney River National Scenic Trail Rides** there. This is a chance to get off the roads and into the woods. Ride well-mannered horses over mountains, through beautiful valleys, along the edge of bluffs, through quiet forests, and along the famous Big Piney River. Rental horses are available for $30 a day plus the regular fee ($30 a day or $150 for six days) and a $50 deposit. Evening entertainment includes horse shows, movies, square dancing, family games, and good wholesome outdoor recreational activities. From May through October the Jerry Laughlin family plans six-day rides. Campsites have a dining hall, modern restrooms, showers, and electricity. Sunday church services are held in a dining hall and on the trail. Arrangements must be made in advance, so call (314) 774–6879, 774–2986, or (800) 742–4679.

The Algonquin Indian word *Montauk* is believed to mean "hilly" (or maybe "fort country," no one is sure). And yes, the Algonquins were settled on the East Coast and Long Island. But this area was settled by homesick easterners in the early 1800s, and they brought the name with them. **Montauk State Park** (314–548–2434) near Licking, east of Lebanon on Highway 32, then south on Highway VV, still has a gristmill with most of its original machinery that was built before the turn of the century. The park is noted for its fine trout fishing in the deep, clear Montauk Springs and in the Current River. There are twenty-five cabins for daily rental during the fishing season (March through October) and a motel with sixteen rooms located in the park.

Wander down Highway VV from Licking and enjoy the rugged countryside, which contains some of the largest springs in the world. The Jacks Fork River, Alley Spring with its restored "Old Red Mill," and the Current River near Eminence provide year-round canoeing. (The spring water is a consistent fifty-eight degrees year round.)

Missouri's southwestern rivers—quick-running, spring-fed, and bone-chillingly cold—are so beautiful they bring a lump to your throat. In fact, the Current, the Eleven Point, and the Jacks Fork have been designated ⊃**Ozark National Scenic Riverways.**

Generations of canoeists and trout fishermen know these secluded waters. You can spend the day without seeing another soul, then camp on a quiet sandbar at day's end and listen to the chuck-will's-widows and owls call while your fire lights the riffles with bronze. Pick fresh watercress from these icy waters to garnish the trout that sizzles in lemon butter on your grill, and know that life gets no better than this. There are plenty of rental outfits; pick up brochures anywhere.

Springs gush from beneath solid rock, slowly carving themselves a cave. Early residents built mills here to produce flour, cornmeal, and sawn lumber. There's as much natural history as history along these bright rivers.

Alley Spring Mill is called the most picturesque spot in the state. Some eighty million gallons of water a day flow through here, and the Red Mill has been restored to working order.

Big Spring is the largest concentration of springs in the world, which is a mystery to hydrologists who do not understand the large volume of water. Beautiful rivers gush right out of the ground from the base of spectacular rock bluffs and create the most consistent, spring-fed, crystal-clear rivers in the country. Round Spring Cave is just off Highway 19.

If you have horses, **Cross Country Trail Rides** has a week planned for you. You can take the whole family on a cross-country trail ride in April, May, June, August, October, or December. Jim and Jane Smith have spent thirty-five years perfecting the week's adventure. You will camp for the week on Jacks Fork River. The ride leaves and returns to the base camp every night, where meals are served and entertainment is royal. Well-known country music performers entertain at a dance every night but Sunday. There are horse shows, team roping events, and other sports to show off your steed. Jane says they fill up months in advance; to ensure a spot, write P.O. Box 15, Eminence 65466, or call (314) 226–3492. The cost is $145 for each adult (lower rates for kids), and there is a $5.00 tie-stall or $10.00 barn-stall reservation for your proud mount. This is a "B.Y.O.H." affair; no rental horses are available.

A winding drive along Highway 160 takes you to the beautiful Eleven Point River, with its many natural springs and lovely spots for picnics. You will be surprised at the excellent roads through these wooded hills. The Between the Rivers section of the Ozark Hiking Trail covers about 30 miles. The northern entry point to this section is on Highway 60 approximately 3½ miles west of Van Buren. Trailhead parking is provided for users at Highway 60 and at Sinking Creek Lookout Tower about a mile west of Highway J.

The trail winds south for the first 13 miles across small tributaries that feed the Current River. Creeks with names such as Wildhorse Hollow, Devil's Run, and Big Barren flow through the area. Designed for both hikers and horses, the trail crosses a ridge that divides the Current River from the Eleven Point River along Gold Mine Hollow. The trail offers panoramic mountain views and deeply wooded areas to filter the summer sun. If you are a hiking enthusiast, this area is for you. Pick up a book with a listing of all the hiking trails on federal property, complete with maps, at the Federal Forest Service Office in Winona, grab your backpack, and head out.

Wooded Ozark roads stretch out before you now, with oak trees shouldering evergreens; the Doniphan Lookout Tower watches the national forest for fires here. Tune your AM radio to 1610 for Ozark Riverway information if you are headed for canoeing or camping at one of the many parks or rivers nearby.

Because of the number of campers who take this route to the wilderness, the little town of Van Buren on Highway 60 is the home of several neat shops. ⊃**Jackie's Country Store** at the corner of Main and John streets is owned by Jackie Wilson, who has lived in Van Buren for almost twenty-three years. "It's a whole different lifestyle," she says of the tiny town. She is from the Kansas City area; now she lives in a house overlooking a river and says she wouldn't live anywhere else. Pick up smoked meats, cheeses, and natural foods as well as deli sandwiches and gifts at this country store.

Jackie has a large pickle jar on the counter and time to chat; the sign on the door says OPEN WHEN I GET HERE, CLOSED WHEN I GET TIRED, and that says something about the lifestyle here. The hours translate to around 9:00 A.M. to 5:00 P.M. (314–323–8560).

⊃**Big Spring Lodge** (314–323–4423) is about 4 miles from Van Buren; it is a National Park Service site on the Ozark National Scenic Riverways. Rustic log cabins with fireplaces that reflect a more relaxed pace and a dining lodge/craft shop were built by the Civilian Conservation Corps (the CCC, otherwise known as "Roosevelt's Tree Army") in the thirties. The lodge is on the National Register, and rightly so; log, timber, rocks, and cut stone materials and unique spatial arrangements make this an excel-lent example of the projects that brought work to so many in Depression-era America. Dining room hours vary with the season. For more information write Big Spring Lodge, P.O. Box 602, Van Buren 63965.

Big Spring State Park is nearby, as are the Mark Twain National Forest and the Ozark National Riverways Tourist Information Station. Brian Culpepper is here to help campers, canoeists, and hikers find what they are looking for; call (314) 323–4236 or write in advance for an accurate list of trails and starting points (P.O. Box 490, Van Buren 63965). Also, any Missouri tourism office can provide a list of hiking trails.

Big Spring is the largest single spring in the world, pouring out 277 million gallons of crystal-clear water each day—a breathtaking natural wonder you will want to photograph or draw.

The beginnings of ⊃**Grand Gulf State Park** (Missouri's answer to the Grand Canyon) in Thayer go back 450 million years to a time when sediment was deposited by ancient seas, forming dolomitic rock. As the area uplifted and the sea receded, water percolated down through cracks in the rock and began to dissolve passageways underneath. Streams cut their own beds on the surface of the soft rock. As air-filled caves formed and cave roofs collapsed, streams were diverted underground. The collapse of the Grand Gulf occurred within the last 10,000 years—fairly recent by a geologist's reckoning.

Today the gulf is ¾ mile wide with side walls 120 feet high. Part of the cave roof that did not collapse formed a natural bridge 75 feet high that spans 200 feet, one of the largest in the state. The park contains handicapped accessible overlooks with spectacular views of the chasm, a ¼-mile loop trail around the gulf, and a primitive trail across the rock bridge (don't look down!). Call (314) 548–2525.

West Plains is a starting point for canoeing on the North Fork River. Or you can strike off on foot into the wilderness of the Mark Twain National Forest.

Travel westbound from West Plains on Highway 160 to Highway 181 north to the little town of Zanoni if you want total peace, quiet, and privacy with nothing to disturb your sleep but the morning song of bluebirds and wrens. The ⊃**Zanoni Mill Inn Bed and Breakfast** is a modern home set beside the remnants of an Ozark pioneer village in a secluded valley with a private lake. It has four large bedrooms, two with connecting baths and two with hall baths. All rooms have queen-size beds, but that is only the beginning of the amenities offered here. How about an 18-by-36 indoor pool and a hot tub where you can soak and watch the big-screen TV? There is ping-pong and pool in the game room. But most interesting is the old mill itself, powered since the Civil War by the spring still gushing out of the hillside, restored and now owned by the great-grandchildren of the original 1870 settlers, and maintained by the grandson of the man who built the present mill in 1905 (the first two burned) to grind corn and wheat. Dave and Mary Morrison turn out a big country breakfast every day, because the home is headquarters of a 1,750-acre working ranch, and that requires a large breakfast, served by the pool if you like. Call (417) 679–4050, or Ozark Mountain Country Reservation Service at (800) 321–8594. Rooms are $60 per night. You might enjoy the Ozark County Old Mill Tour that begins at Zanoni and includes Hodgson, Dawt, Rockbridge, and Hammond Mills. The Morrisons have information on that and on happenings in Branson, as well as fishing possibilities on the North Fork River.

Meander west on Highway 95 to find Rockbridge Mill, where milling began in Ozark County. The town of Rockbridge was burned in the Civil War, but life returned when a small village grew around the 1868 mill. The village is now the **Rainbow Trout Ranch.** A lounge and cafe occupy the old general store. The gristmill and native-stone dam built across the sparkling, spring-fed stream are alive again; the stream wriggles with fat rainbow trout. The original buildings—general store, bank, and church—are restored and provide a delightful setting for a family vacation.

Highways 95 and 14 will take you west to catch Highway 5 North. Or, if back roads are not your thing, continue west on Highway 160 to Dawt Mill (417–284–3540), 12 miles east of Gainsville. The Dawt Mill Lodge, once an old general store and post office at Dawt, Missouri, sleeps two to sixteen. Campsites are available here, too.

North on Highway 5 is tiny Mansfield, home of the ⊃**Laura Ingalls Wilder–Rose Wilder Lane Museum and Home** (417–924–3626). Laura's home is just as she left it; a museum building contains four handwritten manuscripts. Author of the now famous (courtesy of television) *Little House on the Prairie*, among other books, Laura was encouraged to write by her daughter, Rose Wilder Lane, a well-known author in her own right from the early 1900s. They are buried in the Mansfield cemetery.

While in Mansfield, don't miss Jack's Cafe at the corner of Commercial Street and Highway 5–60. It is a good cafe any time, but early in the morning the scent of cinnamon rolls baking wafts through the door. Come in early—they disappear quickly. If you call (417–924–8198), they will set some aside for you.

Laura Ingalls Wilder Home

The **Antique Rose Bed and Breakfast** is in a quaint bungalow near the Wilder home. The country Victorian decor and antiques give the home the right mood, and the hearty country breakfast served at 9:30 will get you going for the day. There are three guest rooms with shared bath as well as a kitchen and sitting area for exclusive guest use for $45. Rooms are available March through November.

The **Dogwood Valley Bed and Breakfast** is near Mansfield just a stone's throw from the Wilder home. This contemporary home has a comfortable great room with fireplace and TV for guests and three elegantly decorated guest rooms, one with a private bath ($60). A delicious breakfast is part of the package. From here you can visit Shapla's Cave (mentioned in the *Little House* books) or hike in the woods, picnic, or fish the ponds. Picnic and dinners can be arranged. For both B&Bs, call Ozark Mountain Country Bed and Breakfast Service, (800) 695–1546.

Go west on Interstate 60 to swing back into Springfield.

Mining Country

Head west on Interstate 44 to Halltown; then slip onto Highway 96 West for Carthage, where the majestic 1895 Jasper County Court House stands proudly on the square, turreted like a medieval castle. Settled in the 1840s, Carthage was burned to the ground in guerrilla raids during the Civil War. Lead and zinc mines were developed after the war and wealthy owners built magnificent homes away from the mining camps. Marble quarries provided Carthage gray marble for many large state and federal buildings. The fine old homes found here bespeak prosperity. It's still a beautiful city—the courthouse, high school, and many of the churches and homes are built of the stone quarried here. (The stone is not technically marble, but a limestone that takes a high polish.) Both the courthouse and high school contain murals by Lowell Davis, one of America's most well-known nature artists and a native of Carthage.

Carthage has more than its share of well-known native sons and is becoming a center for artists in the area. About eighteen resident artists call it home. Internationally known zoologist and naturalist Marlin Perkins (remember "Wild Kingdom"?) was born here; you'll find a bronze sculpture of Perkins by artists Bob Tommey and Bill Snow in Central Park on Garrison Avenue.

Every fall the Midwest Gathering of Artists is held in Carthage, and between 200 and 300 artists come together. There is an auction of works with prices soaring into the thousands of dollars. Call Cindy Higgins for more information about the gathering, at (417) 358–4404.

Follow the historic drive markers for a tour of the magnificent old mansions that have been kept so beautifully over the years. Innkeepers Nolan and Nancy Henry welcome you to their home, the imposing Leggett House, at 1106 Grand (417–358–0683). Nancy and Nolan are from Kansas City. They saw the house, which was in sad repair, and bought it. Nancy says that with their children grown, they needed a hobby—so they moved to Carthage and began restoring the three-story stone mansion. Rates are $45 a night, which includes a full breakfast in the formal dining room.

The Phelps House at 1146 Grand Avenue (417–358–1776) is open for tours from 2:00 P.M. to 5:00 P.M. on Saturdays and Sundays.

⊃**Maple Lane Farm** (417–358–6312), slightly outside of town, is a twenty-two-room Victorian bed and breakfast, complete with animals ranging from horses to pygmy goats to a Sicilian donkey. Arch and Renee (pronounced REE nee) Brewer have seven grown children and many, many grandchildren. Because of the crowd coming home for holidays, the Brewers close at Christmas and Thanksgiving. But the rest of the year their three-story home is open. Deer, turkey, and quail hunting are available. The Brewers offer tours daily at 2:00 P.M. or by appointment. The place is furnished with family heirlooms. Rates are $45 a night with breakfast.

Red Oak II is about 5 miles north of Carthage off of Highway 96. This is the home of Lowell Davis, the Missouri artist/farmer who changes "do-nothing" farm animals into spirited creatures with a world of personality that have caught the imagination of the country. His forty-acre Foxfire Farm was "the ugliest farm in the county" when he and wife Charlie bought it, Davis said in a *Saturday Evening Post* article. It has been transformed into what he calls a "time-warp illusion"; a perfect replica of a thirties farm— buildings, machinery, tools, and all. When Davis goes to shows around the country, he takes a wonderful old huckster's wagon filled with art supplies and memorabilia.

Now Davis has built the town of Red Oak II off of historic Route 66—Missouri Highway 96. Whenever Davis found an old building falling down, he would pick it up and move it to Red Oak, creating a town in a cornfield that feels like his old home town. Now the town has everything you need—church, school, general store, saw mill, feed store, gas station, and blacksmith shop. There are barns, chicken coops (with chickens), corn cribs, old wooden homes surrounded by white picket fences (and privies, of course). It has become a low-key tourist attraction, drawing several dozen people a day. Davis's sculptures and paintings are for sale at the general store, and he has converted four old homes into bed and breakfast inns.

The abandoned tailing piles and mine shafts scattered about the town and the elegant homes just west of the downtown area are reminders of the mining era of Joplin. Mineral collectors are drawn to the abandoned mine dumps and chert piles and to the mineral museum in Schifferdecker Park, one of the best museums of its kind in the state.

But before you start rock hunting in Joplin, stop at ⊃**The Gandy Dancer Bar-B-Que** on Highway 71 South (417–

623–6789). New owner Randal Long has chosen the theme of railroad workers of the late 1800s, who used tools built by the Gandy Company for their rhythmic pounding of the spikes tying the eastern part of the country with the western territories. The meat is still cooked in the carefully planned and home-built smoker that has been turning out incredible slabs of ribs since 1975. The huge stone fireplace warms the rustic cedar building on chilly days. There is a surprise in the men's room—which you fellas will have to discover for yourselves.

Outside Joplin go east on County Highway V to Diamond. From Diamond, drive 2 miles on V and then south about a mile to find the ⊃**George Washington Carver National Monument,** which commemorates a man who was more than an educator, botanist, agronomist, and "cookstove chemist." He was the man who wanted "to be of the greatest good to the greatest number of people," a man who refused to accept boundaries, who drew from science, art, and religion to become a teacher and director of a department at Tuskegee Institute in Alabama. He taught botany and agriculture to the children of ex-slaves and tried to devise farming methods to improve the land exhausted by cotton. Known as the "Peanut Man," Carver led poor, one-horse farmers to grow protein-rich and soil-regenerating soybeans and peanuts. The Carver Nature Trail leads from the birthplace site through two springs and ends at the Carver family cemetery.

Just down Highway 71 is ⊃ **The Real Hatfield Smokehouse** (417–624–3765). Owner Nick Neece has a sparkle in his blue eyes as he talks about his "home-grown" hogs. "We smoke anything you can get from a hog," he says. Bacon, hams—you name it, he smokes it. He will mail hams anywhere in the United States, and even has a regular customer in London. The small smokehouse uses a special sugar cure and hickory logs to give meats a golden brown finish and good flavor without as much salt as other smokehouses. Hours are 7:30 A.M. to 6:00 P.M. seven days a week.

Chugging down Highway 71 toward Neosho will take you right past Doug Hall's ⊃**Log Cabin Store.** What a surprise! Walk inside and find a potbellied stove, three rocking chairs, and Doug and a couple of folks sitting around talking about hunting. An artist by trade, Doug displays his oil paintings among the hunting inventory, archery equipment, muzzle-loading supplies, and coonskin caps. The telephone is unlisted. "I want people to come in and talk to me, not call," he says. And they do.

When you get enough of sitting around indoors, you outdoor folks can go west on Highway 59 at Anderson to enter canoe heaven. Highway 59 runs along the Elk River, and the sudden appearance of the famous overhanging bluffs makes you want to duck as you drive under them.

For over forty years folks have sent cards in bundles to **Noel** (although it's pronounced "Knoll") to have Christmas cards postmarked. Postmaster Bill Poague says they receive about 75,000 cards each December. Stamping is done by volunteers. Parcels should be addressed to Postmaster, Noel, MO 64854. Noel is also the home of the Ozark Wonder Cave, which is on Highway 59 just south of town.

At the intersection of Highway 71–90 in Jane (is there a Tarzan, Missouri nearby?), you will see a rather large log cabin called **The Steak Out** (417–226–4438). It is in the middle of nowhere, but there is a great band in the bar and the kitchen serves a mean steak. It is open seven days a week; owners Orlie and Mindy McCool and Mark and Julie McCool will tell you a little more about the area you are headed into. The lounge opens at 4:00 P.M., restaurant at 5:00 P.M. seven days a week.

Tri-Lakes Area

Cassville is the last town on Highway 76 before you enter the Mark Twain National Forest. It is a long and winding road through the forest, so if you arrive at this point after dark you might as well spend the night. Check out **The Rib** on Highway 112 South (417–847–3600). It's a mighty fine restaurant with a large brick fireplace to ward off the chill. Ron (known as Mack) and Mary Belle McGrath offer a super crisp salad and fine barbecue among other things on the menu.

For breakfast, there is **Dave's Cafe** on Highway 248 East (417–847–3535), where Dave and Pat Kreeger serve homemade bread, pies, and cinnamon rolls. Grits show up on the menu again in this southern latitude, but they serve them with milk and sugar, not butter, on this side of the state. Pat starts baking at 5:30 A.M. and opens at 7:00 A.M. She and Dave serve up fried chicken for $5.00, liver and onions for $3.70, and a menu full of other goodies, all reasonably priced. Winter hours end at 7:00 P.M., but they stay open until 9:00 P.M. during the season. They are open from 8:00 A.M. until 3:00 P.M. on Sunday and are closed on Saturday.

Cassville became the headquarters for the ousted Confederate members of the Missouri General Assembly, and the canyons and steep ridges were great hideouts for bushwhackers. Today the **Mark Twain National Forest** boasts cabins with kitchens and a motel (417–847–2330) as well as campgrounds and a restaurant serving homemade pies, biscuits, and other Ozark goodies during trout season (March through October), when the river is stocked daily.

The ⊃**Devil's Kitchen Trail** winds from the valley to the top and down again, giving a close-up look at the geology and history of the area. Eleven of the park's fourteen caves are found along the rocky bench here. Shelters like these were used by Ozark bluff-dwelling Indians who lived here about 10,000 years ago. Artifacts such as food and fragments of clothing have been found to date this culture. The Devil's Kitchen was named for the stone formation that provided a hideout for Civil War guerrillas. Headed south on Highway 112, softly winding roads, tree-lined hills, and spectacular views pop up as you crest hilltops in this lovely national forest.

⊃**Roaring River State Park** is the fountainhead of the Roaring River. There is a hidden spring in a cave filled with crystal-clear aqua blue water that stays a constant fifty-eight degrees year round. More than twenty million gallons a day are pumped into the river. Here the state maintains a trout hatchery and stocks the river daily in season.

Roaring River State Park is part of the White River basin. From a geologist's point of view, the basin tells a fascinating story. The White River has cut into the flat Springfield plateau, creating deep, steep-walled valleys and exposing varied layers of rock— shale, limestone, dolomite, and chert.

Pastures fringed with woods are found along Highway 76 East through the Piney Creek Wildlife Area. Mile after mile of ridge roads and startling views unfold until finally, over the crest of the last hill, beautiful Table Rock Lake appears before you. It feels like the top of a ferris wheel from this vantage. The occasional small farm or Ozark stone cottage dots the roadside. Valleys with pastures, ponds, or a lone barn sitting starkly against the sky are the only traces of civilization.

At the town of Cape Fair you can turn right on Highway 76 to Table Rock Lake or turn left to Reeds Spring. Because of the proximity of Silver Dollar City, there are quite a few artists in residence. Mark Oehler's ↄ**Omega Pottery Shop** (417–272–3369) on Highway 248 East (at the south edge of town) is one of them. Mark crafts each piece of wheel-thrown stoneware and finishes it in a gas-fired kiln at 2,350 degrees—that makes it safe for oven, dishwasher, microwave, and moon missions. He travels occasionally but says it's "too much of a bother to pack everything up and move it." He would rather stay here in Reeds Spring. "Pottery is a craft that needs space to display it," he says. "That's why potters have studio-galleries."

Mark enjoys doing custom work—such as lamps, sinks, and dishes. He points to other craftspeople—Tom Hess, another potter; Lory Brown, a pine-needle basket maker; Ed Seals, who does copper work; and Kay Cloud and her wonderful Sawdust Doll Houses—all in the Reeds Spring area. Omega Pottery is open from 10:00 A.M. to 5:00 P.M. every day except Wednesday.

At the intersection of Highway 248 and Highway 13 is **Wilderness Road Clockworks and Gallery** (417–272–3256). Floor clocks in a variety of sizes, woods, and styles, including mantel, cuckoo, alarm, and slab clocks, are only a very small part of what this multiroom gift shop offers. Jim Webb is the clock-repair specialist and Pat and Dean Schlobohm run the gift shop, which has dolls, trolls, and wonderful full-size carousel horses. The shop is open from 9:00 A.M. to 5:00 P.M. Monday through Saturday, noon to 5:00 P.M. on Sunday.

Captain Hook's Cove, a luxurious lakefront resort, is designed to meet the needs of handicapped or elderly people. The entire resort was created for the person with limited or non-walking abilities—both indoors and outdoors. It even provides complimentary pontoon boat rides. Captain Mike and his crew, Vicki, Jennifer, and Zack, can be reached at P.O. Box 792, Kimberling City 65686; or call (417) 739–2845 for more detailed information. The cove is situated on Lake Road 00–10.

Table Rock State Park is one of the most popular (meaning crowded) state parks in Missouri. Off the beaten path here means wilderness, on the path means bumper-to-bumper in summertime. As in most resort areas in the state, early spring and late fall are perfect times to roam without the huge crowds summer brings.

Bordering the shore of Table Rock Lake, the park is a popular camping spot in the White River Hills of the Ozarks. Before Silver

Dollar City (long, long before—say 10,000 years ago) Indians inhabited the area. Bluff Dwellers, who were "new kids on the block" 3,000 years ago, left artifacts now dated by modern anthropologists. Trappers and hunters roamed the hills, and in 1818 Henry Rowe Schoolcraft wrote of the wonders of this area. Settlers began to arrive in the early 1800s from North Carolina and Tennessee, and because of the area's resemblance to their southern Appalachian Mountain homes, they decided to stay. The division between the anti-slavery farmers and those who were Confederate supporters slashed the state here as it did everywhere else, and vigilante groups such as the "Baldknobbers" roamed the area.

Author Harold Bell Wright came to these hills for his health in the early part of this century and was so taken by the beauty of the area that he settled in to write. *The Shepherd of the Hills* is his best-known and most-beloved book; it captured the imagination of generations and even became one of John Wayne's early movies (which, incidentally, borrowed only the name from the book—the script was unrecognizable!).

Shepherd of the Hills country became a visitors' attraction nearly seventy years ago, with its site based on Wright's book. Old Matt's Cabin (named after the book's patriarchal character), its outbuildings, and neighboring buildings—Sammy Lane's home, Aunt Molly's Kitchen, and the old post office—were the first attractions in the area.

The outdoor theater at the Shepherd of the Hills seats about 8,000 people. It is more than just a theater, however; horses ride through, the audience helps put out burning cabins, and with a thirty-year run, Shepherd of the Hills has outrun anything ever on Broadway, with production values that make you believe that cabin's on fire. The play runs May through October. There is a special Nativity play during the Christmas season. (The Nativity play features wise men with Ozark accents and has a flavor all its own.)

Highway 65 is an old-fashioned, uncrowded Ozark highway. You can still see the view as you crest hills here, but the ⊃**Shepherd of the Hills Inspiration Tower** offers an incredible one. The tower's first observation level is at 145 feet; the tower is 230 feet, 10 inches tall, with two elevators or 279 stairs to the top. But rest assured it is stable. It is designed to withstand 172 mph winds (gusts of 224 mph) and it cost $1.5 million to build;

this is not surprising since it contains 92,064 pounds of steel and is set in forty-three truckloads of concrete. It also contains 4,400 square feet of glass, for a breathtaking view from the highest point around the Tri-Lake area.

If you've heard of Silver Dollar City (and you will if you stay in Missouri for long), you've heard of Branson. Once a quiet little town pocketed in the weathered Ozark Mountains near the Arkansas border, business here has picked up considerably.

Branson has changed in the last few years from the strip of country music "opries" and related foofaraw crowded cheek-by-jowl along Highway 76 to the country music capital of the Midwest, giving Nashville a run for its money. Twenty-seven theaters in town now feature such stars as Johnny Cash, Loretta Lynn, Andy Williams, Mel Tillis, and Roy Clark, who join regulars such as Boxcar Willie, Moe Bandy (the show President Bush and his staff stopped to see after the '92 GOP convention), and possibly the most popular show in town, Japanese hillbilly fiddler Shoji Tabuchi.

Branson is trying to keep up with the demand of more than four million tourists a year, but as you would suspect, about an hour before the matinee or evening shows begin, the traffic is much like a long narrow parking lot. How bad is the traffic? Well, women have been seen leaving their husbands behind the wheel on Highway 76 while they get out and shop, buy things, and rejoin their spouses in the car a block or so up the street. We are talking gridlock here. The secret to getting around is learning the back roads. Just knowing that the quickest route from Andy Williams' Theater to Ray Stevens' is Forsythe Street to Truman to Shepherd of the Hills Expressway—and not 76 Country Boulevard (a road to avoid if at all possible)—can save you enough time for dinner.

There are other little secrets, too. The Chamber of Commerce will give you a free, easy-to-read map showing the shortcuts from one end of the 5-mile strip to the other. The recently repaved back roads can make life a little easier, even though you can't avoid the traffic altogether. The city is testing a trolley system on the strip, but for now it's face the traffic or walk. (Disney scouts have been looking at land around Branson for a theme park, too. That should make things even more interesting.)

The most exciting part of visiting Branson is how easy it is to get up close to the stars, the music legends who are playing golf

(10:00 A.M. on Wednesday at Pointe Royale Golf Course on Highway 165 often has Mel Tillis, Andy Williams, Moe Bandy, and Boxcar Willie teeing off together) or shopping at the grocery store. That constellation of stars is only the beginning. Also building a theater in Branson is Wayne Newton. Other stars scheduled to shoot through Branson for performances are Larry Gatlin, Kenny Rogers, Reba McEntire, illusionist David Copperfield, Marie Osmond, and Marilyn McCoo.

So you never know whom you will see sitting in one of the many restaurants (most of which are down-home sorts of places, not exactly low-calorie eating places) in town. But for the best ambience, drive across the lake to the **Candlestick Inn** on Mt. Branson on East Seventy-sixth Street, where the food is more upscale. The atmosphere is romantic, the view of downtown Branson is sensational (especially during the Christmas season's Festival of Lights), and you never know who will be at one of the tables. The menu features such delicacies as crab-stuffed trout. You can see the humongous neon candle (says "steak and seafood") sign from downtown, but it's tricky to find if you don't know to just follow Highway 76–68 across the bridge. Call (417)334–3633 for reservations.

Now, beyond the music shows and Silver Dollar City, there are a few other places worth seeing. **Mutton Hollow Craft Village** is a smaller and less expensive version of Silver Dollar City near 76 Country Boulevard and Shepherd of the Hills Expressway. There are thirty-eight shops, where crafters make things the way they did one hundred years ago. You can eat barbecued ribs cooked over an open pit and enjoy the evening variety show for $7.95; it promises to be over by 7:00 so you can make the evening shows at the nearby theaters. Admission is $4.95; children four to eleven, $2.85.

Needless to say, there are many motels around Branson. You can escape the motel rut with a bed and breakfast if you plan ahead a little. Plus, the people in the B&Bs tend to know their way around the town and can give you the shortest, fastest routes to wherever you are planning to go. **Call Ozark Mountain Country Bed and Breakfast Service** at (800) 695–1546 and let Kay Cameron find you one of the more than thirty-five B&Bs in the Tri-Lakes area near Table Rock Lake, Lake Taneycomo, Branson, or Silver Dollar City or just across the border in Arkansas. She has about a hundred bed and breakfast inns to direct you to in the

63

Ozarks. Kay also has the number of a ticket service that will deliver tickets to any bed and breakfast inn for you.

The easiest way to reach Branson is from Highway 65, which runs through the east end of town. The West Missouri 76 exit will put you on the strip, where you will watch pedestrians speed by your slowly moving car. Or you can use the back entrance and take Highway 248 to the Shepherd of the Hills Expressway to the west side of town, where things will not be much better. You can reach the Branson/Lakes Area Chamber of Commerce at (900) 884–BRANSON for a guide that lists the shows in town and the ticket office phone numbers. There is a $1.50 per minute charge for that call (average three minutes) and you get a recording to leave your name and address. It is sometimes cheaper to call the visitor information number at (417) 334–4136, but that line is often busy and you can be put on hold for about ten minutes. They have a computerized service listing the hotels and motels with vacant rooms. For show tickets you can call BransonTix, a private company that handles about a dozen theaters, at (800) 888–8497.

Do flea markets interest you? You're in the right place—downtown Branson has five of them. If you don't find something in this lineup, you aren't looking very hard, or you have a good deal more self-discipline than most of us!

The ⊃**Stone Hill Wine Company** (417–334–1897), located on Highway 165 2 blocks south of Highway 76 West, is open Monday through Saturday 8:30 A.M. to 6:00 P.M. and noon to 6:00 P.M. on Sunday for cellar tours and wine tasting. Stone Hill makes mead, which is a honey wine made since ancient times. Couples in England were given a month's supply of mead as a wedding gift. The period in which they drank the wine became known as the "honeymoon" (now there's a piece of information you can surely use somewhere). The gift shop sells sausages and cheese made at the winery. Owners Jim and Betty Held also own the winery in Hermann.

An English village in the heart of Ozark mountain country? Unlikely, but true. Just across the bridge on Highway 65 sits little ⊃**Hollister,** a quaint Tudor getaway less crowded than neighboring Branson.

Ye Olde Iron Kettle Food and Drink is owned by Rosalea Whitehorn. Hollister is a sleepy little town in winter, but the population swells by three and a half million in the Branson area when summer comes, says Bonnie Hoover, manager of the Kettle. Many people seek out the Hollister Hotel to avoid the crowds across the river.

Slow down 2 miles outside of town and turn west on Highway V. There's something here you won't want to miss: the ⊃**School of the Ozarks** (417–334–9961 or –6411) in Point Lookout.

It's a college campus, all right, but wait! What's going on here? Everybody looks so . . . *busy*. This is a different kind of college—a fully accredited, four-year school where each full-time boarding student works at one of sixty-five campus jobs or industries to pay in part for his or her tuition. It calls itself "the campus that works." The rest is provided through scholarships. The campus fruitcake and jelly kitchen is open during business hours weekdays. Student workers bake some 20,000 fruitcakes a year and produce delicious apple butter and many flavors of jelly.

Students built the college itself—it's a pretty one—and run the Ralph Foster Museum and the Edwards Mill (a working replica of an old-time gristmill) as part of their tuition. If you're hungry while you're here, stop at the student-run Friendship House and Gift Shop. It's an all-you-can-eat smorgasbord where the little ones under five can eat for free—can you pass it up? You can get a mighty prime steak here, they tell us. Friendship House is open between 7:00 A.M. and 7:30 P.M. Monday through Saturday and Sunday until 3:30 P.M.

The campus is beautiful, perched on its hill; don't miss the view from Point Lookout. Stand here at dusk when the bell carillon rolls out over the mist-shrouded river below, if you want goosebumps up and down your arms. When the sun slides down the sky, that sound of bells on the crisp evening air is unforgettable. Williams Memorial Chapel is a fine place to stop for a moment; the tourist bustle slows to a halt here and there's room to breathe.

Ozark Vineyard Winery at Highway 65 and Highway 176 West in Chestnutridge is 10 miles north of Branson. Owner and wine master Herschel Gray uses grapes from the Mountain Grove area to make his unusual wines. His Bonnie Brook Wine is a white wine aged in old whiskey barrels, giving it the unusual nutty combination of flavors captured from the charcoal of the scorched barrels, the bourbon, and the wood.

This you have to see to believe. ⊃**Cathedral Church of the Prince of Peace** is the world's smallest cathedral. Situated in

Peace Cathedral

Highlandville, it's 3 miles off Highway 65 and 1,500 yards off Highway 160 (take County Road EE to Highlandville.) It is the cathedral of the very, very small Christ Catholic Church, which claimed the title of "the Catholic Peace Church" in 1965. Beautiful cathedral gardens with many varieties of geraniums surround the Ozark-stone building, which looks like a tiny garage. But walk right up there and open the door. Inside is a cathedral—complete with pews, candles, altar, tabernacle, and prie-dieu. Mass is every morning at 11:00 A.M., and a litany for peace is offered every day. Bishop Karl Pruter is the presiding bishop. Built of native stone, the cathedral is 14 by 17 feet and seats a congregation of fifteen; it is mentioned in the *Guinness Book of Records*. The blue cupola (onion dome) suggests the church's Eastern rite affiliation. Bishop Pruter suggests knocking on the door of the house attached to the church by a covered walkway if you want to talk about the Catholic Peace Church. Call (417) 587–3951.

Just a mile east of Highway 65 on Highway 14, the town of ↄ**Ozark** is a haven for antiques buffs. The largest collection is housed at the **Maine Streete Mall,** a warehouse along Highway

65 and home to 108 antiques dealers. There are even antique cars inside. In the same area **Apple Jacks Craftsman's Mall** and **Crossroad Antiques** also are filled with a gazillion items. But a trip to Ozark itself will find dozens more shops. This town, 15 miles south of Springfield and near enough to Branson to draw its crowds, is a Mecca for folks who love old stuff. Susan Marler, owner of **Touches of Tyme Antique Store** at 103 West Church (417–485–0671) can give you a list of all of the shops in town and will even call around for you to find what you want if her shop doesn't have it. But you won't be in a hurry to leave her building, because along with the antiques shop, it is home to a couple of other interesting places. **Silver Linings** (417–485–0485) is Anne Scott's dress shop. But it's not just a dress shop; Anne is a fashion design teacher at Southwest Missouri State University in Springfield and designs the Victorian and country clothing sold in her shop. Both shops are open from 10:00 A.M. until 4:30 P.M. Then you can stop in for something to eat at the **Highland** (417–485–0102), Sara Carr's and Rita Wright's tea room. Pastas, salads, and other homemade luncheon specials are on the menu. The tea room is open from 11:00 A.M. until 3:00 P.M.; all three shops are open every day but Sunday.

Country View Bed and Breakfast is near the town of Nixa. This charming country home is filled with antiques, and the full country breakfast is served on antique china. A romantic queen-size canopy bed, private bath, and sitting room are yours for $55. Other rooms with twin beds and shared bath are $40. Call Ozark Mountain Country Bed and Breakfast Service for reservations, (800) 695-1546.

Turn west at Nixa and if your sweet tooth is deviling you, find ↄ**Ye Olde Nixa Mercantile and Sweet Shoppe** in a charming 1909 building at 107 South Main Street. It is open Monday through Saturday from 9:00 A.M. to 5:00 P.M. and is filled with country clothing and collectibles.

On the road back to Springfield check out the **Vermillion Factory Outlet** (417–744–2058) in Billings, which features oak and walnut items—cutting boards, wine racks, and butcher-block tables. There is even a bargain room with scrap boxes for crafts-people and woodworkers. Located on Highway 60 southwest of Springfield, the outlet is open from 8:00 A.M. to 4:30 P.M. Monday through Friday, 9:00 A.M. to 5:00 P.M. Sunday (March through December).

Wilson's Creek National Battlefield is 3 miles east of Republic on Highway ZZ, south of Springfield. A battle for Missouri's Union allegiance was fought here in 1861. The visitors' center features a film, or you can watch living history demonstrations at the Ray House and Bloody Hill on weekends during the summer.

Off the Beaten Path in Central Missouri

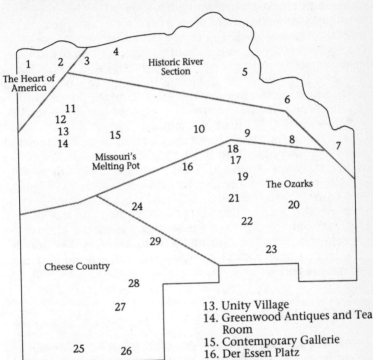

The Heart of America

1 2 3 4

Historic River Section

5

6

11
12
13
14

15

Missouri's Melting Pot

10

9

8

7

18
17

16

19

The Ozarks

21

20

22

24

29

23

Cheese Country

28

27

25 26

1. Steamboat *Arabia* Museum
2. Clinton's
3. Fort Osage
4. Anderson House State Historic Site
5. Arrow Rock
6. Thespian Hall
7. Jefferson Landing
8. Burgers' Smokehouse
9. Dutch Bakery and Bulk Food Store
10. Bothwell State Park
11. Powell Gardens
12. Missouri Town 1855

13. Unity Village
14. Greenwood Antiques and Tea Room
15. Contemporary Gallerie
16. Der Essen Platz
17. Lehmans'
18. Kurtz General Store
19. Pleasant Valley Quilts and Tea Room
20. Orr Gallery and Studio
21. Spring Lake Lodge and Antiques
22. Old Trail House
23. Ha Ha Tonka State Park
24. Henry County Museum
25. Harry S Truman's Birthplace
26. Golden Prairie
27. Bush Hotel
28. Stockton Cheese Shop
29. Colby's Cafe

Central Missouri

Welcome to America's Heartland, where the Mighty Mo marks the end of the glaciated plains, and hill country begins. Remnant prairies tucked between the hills remind us that once these seas of grass covered a third of the state. In this area there are not one but three big lakes, and from Kansas City to the Lake of the Ozarks lie tiny towns built on gentle ridges, waiting to be discovered. Rough gravel roads wind through dogwood forests, along tentacled lakeshores and into towns that seem to have been protected from the rush like the wild morel hidden under a leaf. The big city here is Kansas City: the birthplace of jazz, the homeland of barbecue, and the Heart of America.

The Lake of the Ozarks is not only a tourist area, it is a second-home site for people from both Kansas City and St. Louis. The eastern lakeshore, known as the St. Louis side, has million-dollar homes in the Land of the Four Seasons Resort area. Six Mile Cove (the six-mile marker means you are six miles from Bagnell Dam) is called Millionaires' Cove by people cruising the lake by boat and has some of the most opulent homes in the Midwest. A houseboat business has sprung up on that side, and visitors can now cruise the lake and see both shores without the long drive around the lake.

The Heart of America

Describing **Kansas City** as a city with "manure on its feet and wheat in its jeans" was fair at one time. Its two major industries were meat and wheat—all because a man named Joe McCoy convinced the local powers-that-were in 1871 that the newfangled "bobwire" made it impossible to herd Texas cattle east. A central shipping point was needed, and the Kansas City stockyard was born (where a fine steakhouse, the Golden Ox, is within sniffing distance at 1600 Genessee).

Kansas City is known as the "Heart of America," not because of its location in the center of the country, but because of the people who call it home. Kansas City has a symphony, a lyric opera, the Missouri State Ballet Company, Royals baseball, and the Kansas City Chiefs. Enclosed in the very heart of the city is Swope Park, the second-largest city park in the nation, with quiet, tree-shaded picnic areas and a modern zoo on the way to being upgraded to world-class.

The Nelson-Atkins Museum owns one of the finest collections of Oriental art in the world and has a beautiful outdoor sculpture garden. The Kansas City Museum has a planetarium and an old-fashioned ice-cream parlor where you can order a phosphate or a sundae. The Kansas City studio of artist Thomas Hart Benton is now a state park.

The first question most visitors ask when they get off a plane at the Kansas City International Airport is, "Where's the best barbecue?" That's up for grabs—you be the judge. The oldest contenders are **Rosedale Barbecue** at 632 Southwest Boulevard, **Arthur Bryant Barbecue** at 1727 Brooklyn, and **Gates and Sons Bar-B-Q** at 1411 Swope Parkway. All offer carryout, so you can do comparison tests until you are all "pigged out."

Here and there, drowsing on old streets, pocketed in small shopping centers, crouching behind buildings, or even tucked inside buildings, you're likely to find places that definitely qualify as out of the mainstream.

Downtown (*way* downtown) is the **City Market,** where you can shop outdoors with a big wicker basket for just-picked produce in the wonderful atmosphere of a European marketplace. You can buy everything from morel mushrooms in early May to late-harvest turnips in October. There are always fresh eggs and chickens, and on Saturday mornings local farmers and buyers meet over the freshest produce this side of the garden. The area hard by the Missouri River has undergone restoration, complete with a riverboat museum. Rumor has it that now that riverboat gambling has been approved by taxpayers and millions of dollars in redevelopment money are about to be invested, the area will soon become as busy as it was when Kansas City was young.

The year was 1856 when the steamboat *Arabia* set out for the West, loaded with trade goods and passengers. As the folks at the ƆSteamboat *Arabia* Museum say, you'll find axes, awls, and augers to zillions of other treasures restored to near-mint condition. How did they manage to amass all this in one place? Well, the *Arabia* hit a cottonwood snag in the Missouri River and sank like a stone. There it rested from 1856 to 1988, a time capsule waiting to spill its treasures both everyday and exotic into the present. But of course, even the everyday from over one hundred years ago is exotic now. You'll find spurs, tinware, perfume (that retained its scent after its sojourn under 45 feet of mud and water), wine, whiskey, and champagne (still bubbly), canned goods, hair pins, inkwells, and clothing.

The Hawley family excavated the boat and spent untold hours painstakingly restoring the artifacts they found. To our good fortune, they opened a museum rather than selling off the bounty, and this treasure trove now tells historians, living-history reenactors, and just plain history buffs volumes about what life was like on the frontier; civilization was built with the bits and pieces of trade goods carried by packets like the *Arabia*. A short film introduces you to the museum and to the excavation and restoration process. See what frontier life was like for $5.50 for adults, $5.00 for seniors, $3.25 for children four to twelve; younger kids are free. Hours are Tuesday through Saturday, 10:00 A.M. to 6:00 P.M. and Sunday from noon to 5:00 P.M.; for information call (816) 471–4030.

Inside the Fifth Street market building is **Cascone's Grill,** where the market crowd eats. The Cascone family cooks up the most amazing early-morning Italian breakfasts (Italian breaded steak, fried eggs, hash browns, and Italian bread toast) and late-in-the-day lunches featuring Vita Cascone's own spaghetti sauce. They open and close seasonally with the rhythm of the market crowd.

Catty-corner from the market, across the street at 513 Walnut, is **Planters' Seed.** Step inside this old building and inhale the wonderful odors of fresh bulk herbs and spices, the scent of old wood, the aroma of exotic teas and coffees, and the clean smell of seeds. Need a watering can? They've got 'em. Want to buy a pound of dried bay leaves? Look no further. It's a delightful place.

Just south of the busy interstates that ring downtown Kansas City proper is **Central Park Gallery** at 1644 Wyandotte (816–471–7711); it's a newly renovated, 108-year-old, three-story schoolhouse. Brenda and Jim Miles bought the old grade school and converted it into a showcase of midwestern fine art, highlighting lithographs, raku ware, and original paintings. A bit farther south is **Central Park Gallery II** in the Crown Center Shops, a complex of small boutiques in and around Crown Center. Call (816) 471–7744 for directions or enjoy poking around the shops that range from ethnic to outrageous.

Moving south, slow up at the old Union Station. Tucked under the wings of the station is **Creative Candles** (816–474–9711) at 330 West Pershing Road (look sharp or you'll miss it—just past the main post office on Pershing make a hard right and go down below street level). Creative they are indeed. Duane Benton got into the candle business in the sixties like a lot of other idealistic entrepreneurial dropouts; the difference is that Duane kept at it and now sells candles throughout the United States.

Union Station Annex is the place to board the *Ann Rutledge* or the *Mule,* two of Amtrak's red-white-and-blue-striped silver trains that will take you through the Missouri River Valley to St. Louis at speeds of 70 mph. Through flat farmland and into the rolling, wooded Missouri hill country, the scenery is beautiful any time of the year. But the special time for this ride is in the fall when the blaze of color flanks the river's startlingly white limestone bluffs. Every weekend in October, Amtrak schedules special stops in Hermann for the Octoberfest, when the air is filled with polka music and the smell of grilled bratwursts. Then the train passes through Washington along Front Street and into Kirkwood. It's about a five-hour trip one way and departs Kansas City at 9:15 A.M. with a stop in Independence and Lee's Summit. Round-trip coach tickets are $45. Call (800) USA–RAIL for details.

In parts of the city some fine old mansions still sit shaded by oak trees planted when the city was young. **Milford House,** at 3605 Gilham Road, is over a hundred years old and still a beauty. Now it is a bed and breakfast . . . (816) 753–1269; the owners' British accents are as elegant as Milford House itself.

Historic Westport, some 40 blocks south of downtown, was the whole city at one time. Some of us think it still is. Check out **The Classic Cup** (816–756–0771) at 4130 Pennsylvania, owned by Charlene Welling. Originally *the* spot in Kansas City for gourmet coffee beans, it now offers a selection of imported cheeses, pâté, and preserves. The bakery, ruled by pastry chef Paul Frazier, offers incredible edibles.

The Cup now runneth over; you can pick from one of the finest wine lists in the city and stay for a wonderful lunch. Chef Brenda Sweeny is the creative engine behind the apron. The menu changes daily but is always based on fresh ingredients.

The all-time favorite entree is the Raspberry-Dijon Mustard Sauce on Grilled Pork Tenderloin (sometimes it's blueberry, blackberry, or tart cherry Dijon sauce). Hours are Monday through Thursday from 10:00 A.M. to 6:00 P.M., Friday and Saturday from 10:00 A.M. to 10:00 P.M., and Sunday from 11:00 A.M. to 5:00 P.M. (with a Sunday brunch from 11:00 A.M. to 2:00 P.M.).

Let's get small. If you love tiny things (or if you haven't quite grown up), don't miss the **Toys and Miniatures Museum** at 5235 Oak Street (816–333–2055). Mary Harris Francis and Barbara Marshall started the museum on a small scale, but its new 14,000-square-foot addition gives them plenty of room for little stuff. There are over eighty-five antique furnished dollhouses at least one hundred years old, scale-model miniature rooms, and boys' toys. The museum is open Wednesday through Saturday 10:00 A.M. to 4:00 P.M. and Sunday from 1:00 P.M. to 4:00 P.M. It is closed for two weeks following Labor Day.

Of course, in cities the size of Kansas City there is something for everyone if you know where to look. Sometimes just finding the first place is the key. For example, if your taste leans to designer clothes but your money leans more toward off-the-rack, you might enjoy browsing in some of K.C.'s consignment shops. After pricing new clothes on the Country Club Plaza, check out **My Sister's Closet** at 1201 West Forty-seventh Street just 3 blocks west of the Plaza. There sisters Mary Ellison and Michelle Donnelly have a boutique where you will discover Plaza style at much better prices—everything from silk blouses to fur coats. They also have a list of the eleven other consignment shops in the Kansas City area (816–531–0067). Hours are Monday through Friday from 10:00 A.M. until 6:00 P.M. and Saturday until 5:00 P.M.

South of the Country Club Plaza, in Brookside, in an old Texaco station, is a small wine bar and cafe called **Joe D's** (6227 Brookside Plaza). It was the first wine bar in the country. Owner Joe DiGiovanni, one of the leaders of Les Amis du Vin (Friends of Wine), is a personable young man who will sit down and talk wine anytime.

He has the largest by-the-glass wine list in Kansas City and his house wines are excellent. His menu changes each day, depending on what seasonal fresh produce and meat the chef has discovered. Unusual entrees such as Breast of Chicken with Strawberry Peppercorn Sauce, Orange Cream Fettucini, or Fresh Marlin with Coconut Banana Curry Sauce are written on a chalkboard. The pizza du jour on fresh Italian Baboli bread (artichoke and crab pizza? Yes!) changes with the chef's mood. Joe D's (816–333–6116) opens weekdays at 11:30 A.M. and closes at midnight; Saturdays it is open from 5:00 P.M. until 1:30 A.M. After dinner be sure to try Joe's bread pudding with hot caramel sauce, just like grandma used to make. Entrees range from about $8.00 to $18.00.

Narrow oak floorboards, narrow aisles, and broad, broad choices—that's what you expect from an old-fashioned dime store. And that's what you get at **The Dime Store,** just around the corner from Joe D's on Sixty-third Street. There's not all that much you can get for a dime anymore, but you can find anything from barrettes to bushel baskets here. It's been in the same family since the late thirties, and serves the old neighborhood as it always did.

Joanne and Jack Clingenpeel opened **Wild Birds Unlimited** at 10143 Wornall (816–942–4887) to serve the needs of these wild creatures and the folks who love them. You'll find all you'll ever need to know about attracting and feeding birds, plus feeders, houses, waterers, and seed. A raisin suet cake smelled good enough to eat—only the cholesterol count prevented us from taking a bite! The Clingenpeels have a photo contest every year and keep listings of bird sightings.

The city of Independence, just east of downtown Kansas City on Interstate 70, could be a day trip in itself: There's Harry S Truman's home, now a national park, and the Truman Presidential Library; the RLDS Auditorium, world center for the Reorganized Church of Latter Day Saints; and Civil War battlefields. Here you'll find the beginnings of the Santa Fe Trail, still visible in the worn earth. (Sometimes it seems as if half the towns on this side of the state claim the trail, but in Independence they still celebrate the Santa-Cali-Gon, where the Santa Fe, California, and Oregon trails jumped off into the wilderness.) The recently opened National Frontier Trails Center is a fine place to learn more about the hardships and adventures of those who dared to leave civilization behind and strike out across the wilderness to a new life. It's in the historic Waggoner-Gates Milling Company building. Call (816) 254–0059 for further information.

There are antiques stores, B&Bs, and dandy places to eat—in short, there's entirely too much to include in a single volume. We've narrowed it down to these few, which are off the beaten path by virtue of location, and arcane historical significance, or ambience.

Don't miss ⊃**Clinton's** on the square, at 100 West Maple. When he was on the campaign train in Independence, President Bill Clinton visited here; they have photos and a thank-you letter to prove it! (He has a Clinton's sweatshirt.) Just how long has it been since you've had a real chocolate soda or cherry phosphate? While you're there, ask them to make a chocolate-cherry cola; it's like a liquid, chocolate-covered cherry with a twist. This is a real old-time soda fountain, complete with uniformed soda jerks and a marble counter with a mirrored back; the malts still whir in those tall, frosty metal cans like they did when we were kids. (816) 813–2625.

And if all this hedonistic revelry doesn't get you, maybe the historical angle will: Truman's very first job was at Clinton's. You don't *have* to be a jerk first to be President, but maybe it helps. Harry was one of our most popular commanders-in-chief.

You think celebrity prisoners in our jails are pampered *now*. When Frank James was held at the jail in Independence, his cell sported an Oriental carpet; he had guests in for dinner and served them fine wines. For that matter, so did William Quantrill when he was incarcerated here.

Although the dank cells with their monolithic stone walls were decorated when company called, they were still jail. A hundred and thirty years after the fact, the cells are still dark, forbidding holes that look impossible to escape. The **Old Jail Museum** and **Marshall's Home** (816–252–1892) are at 217 North Main.

Perhaps you remember the nineteenth-century painting of two trappers in a long wooden canoe. A big black animal—perhaps a cat, perhaps a bear—sits in the bow gazing enigmatically at the viewer. Or maybe "The Jolly Boatmen" is more your style, with the rivermen dancing at the dock, playing instruments, and generally raising a ruckus. Artist George Caleb Bingham painted both, along with many others depicting life along the Western Frontier.

Bingham made his home for a time at the elegant **Bingham-Waggoner Estate** at 313 West Pacific, where he watched two Civil War battles rage across his front lawn (not conducive to painting a decent picture. Think what that would do to your concentration!).

Visit from April to October, Monday through Saturday from 10:00 A.M. till 4:00 P.M. to find out how the "other half" lived in the last century—or rent the mansion for a festive event and make the past your own. The mansion is also open from late November through December for the Christmas season; they decorate all twenty-six rooms. Fee is $2.50 for adults, $2.00 for senior citizens, and 50 cents for children under twelve, with slightly higher winter fees to defray the cost of all those decorations. Call (816) 461–3491.

The **Woodstock Inn Bed and Breakfast** at 1212 West Lexington (816–833–2233) offers comfort, privacy, and hospitality. Each of the eleven guest rooms has its own private bath. Mona and Ben Crosby are the managers. Rates are from $40 to $65. If you are traveling with a family, try the suite with a queen-size bed and an extra sitting room that can sleep four comfortably for $65 for two and $7.50 for each additional person.

A maze of interstates has left old Highway 40 very nearly off the beaten path. Find the highway just south of the intersection of Noland Road and Interstate 70, and turn east to **Stevenson's Apple Orchard and Restaurant** at Lee's Summit Road; this one is well worth a stop, as happy eaters from presidents to movie stars have discovered. A large barrel of their famous cider keeps waiting diners happy. Stevenson's is sprawling but done in small rooms to keep the feeling intimate; some rooms are elegant, others are like dining in a rustic wine cellar. Enjoy an apple daiquiri (or peach or strawberry in season) and their famous smoked chicken. Meals are served with almost too many choices (savory green rice, frozen fruit salad, several types of muffins, and Stevenson's own apple fritters). Call (816) 373–5400 for reservations.

And two blocks east of Stevenson's is one of the dandiest antiques malls you'll ever want to explore—**Country Meadows** (816–373–0410), at 4621 Schrank Drive (don't worry, you can see it from Highway 40). It's huge, upstairs and downstairs; plan on taking plenty of time.

An antiques mall is an antiques mall is an antiques mall, right? Not in this case. There's also a tea room, if you get hungry; if a powerful thirst is upon you and you just need a treat, there's an old-fashioned soda fountain adjacent to the tea room.

Exclusively Missouri is Donna Leker's shop inside the mall, offering gifts from all over the state of Missouri, from herbs to quilts to figurines to good old hard candies; if you have a special need, reach her at (816) 373–5767.

Devotees of buckskinning, rendezvous, and living history will love Ed and C.J. Wilde's shop in the southwest corner of the mall, which offers everything from C.J.'s wonderful hand-woven blankets and Ed's own period leather goods to knives made from flint and antler, muzzle-loading guns, Peter Goebel's copperware, clothing for the historic reenactor, period musical tapes, and all sorts of goodies. The Wilde's shop looks like a trading post from frontier Missouri—and that's just what it is, the twentieth century notwithstanding.

Historic River Section

How about a day trip back in time? It's 1803, the year of the Louisiana Purchase: Imagine Missouri nearly empty of "civilization," as it was when it became part of the United States. Early fur trappers traded necessities—like tobacco, tomahawks, blankets, fabrics, and cookware. The Osage peoples were the most common Indians in this area, and they did business amicably with both French and American trading posts.

East of Independence you'll explore ⊃**Fort Osage,** a National Historic Landmark and the westernmost U.S. outpost in the Louisiana Purchase; its site was chosen by Lewis and Clark; construction was originally supervised by William Clark himself. Strategically overlooking the Missouri River, the fort was reconstructed from detailed plans preserved by the U.S. War Department and it stands today on its original foundation. Artifacts unearthed during the excavation are on display.

You may find a living history reenactment in progress, complete with trappers and military men, Indians, storytellers, and musicians. Costumes are authenticated down to the last bit of fringe, and guides learn their alter egos' life and times so thoroughly that you forget you are only visiting the past. Sit inside a real tipi, watch arrowheads being made from local flint, or visit the trading post to purchase unique gift items with a sense of history (like real bone buttons).

Rustle up a group to enjoy one of the after-hours programs offered by Jackson County Heritage Program. You can reserve a place at a hearthside supper in the factor's dining rooms, for example. Enjoy an authentic nineteenth-century meal by candlelight; then cozy up to the fireplace and savor the entertainment.

Several weekends a year, special events like the Sheep Shearing (May), Frontier Festival (June), or Militia Muster and Candlelight Tour (October) are offered, or spend the Fourth of July as our forebears did—the fort's a great place for it.

Fort Osage

To find Fort Osage (816–249–5737), take Highway 24 from Kansas City east to Buckner and turn north at Sibley Street (Highway BB); follow the gray signs through the tiny town of Sibley. Weekend activities are 9:00 A.M. till 5:00 P.M., but you can explore on your own Wednesday through Sunday from April till November. Admission is $3.00 for adults and $1.00 for children five through thirteen and senior citizens. Children four and under are free.

A more historic (and scenic) route between Fort Osage and Lexington will take you down the Highway 224 spur through Napoleon, Waterloo, and Wellington. This is Lafayette County—beginning to get the picture here? Must have been history buffs around this area since dirt was young. The road runs along the Missouri River, sometimes almost at water level, other times from a spectacular river-bluff view.

Don't miss the turnoff to tiny downtown Napoleon; it's a lovely place to pick up a bit of lunch in a real old-fashioned general store. The **G&S General Store** celebrated its centennial in 1992. This is no upscale yuppie fern bar; you'll find hardware, horse liniment, and canned goods on the aisles leading back to the deli area. And what a deli—it's an old-time meat case where owners will make you a sandwich while you wait—maybe a fresh pink pastrami on rye with the works. A big case full of soft drinks, milk, and juices completes the offerings.

Across the street is **Ma & Pa's Riverview Antique Mall** (816–934–2698), and they're not kidding about the view—it's wonderful. The Missouri River shines like a mirror far below, and rich bottomland fields fill the rest of the space to the far hills. Harold and Betty Reaves welcome you Monday through Saturday 9:30 A.M. to 5:30 P.M. and Sunday noon to 6:00 P.M.

A bit farther on is Waterloo, just between Napoleon and Wellington—the obvious place, don't you think? There's not much here but a sign and a few houses, but it would be perfect even if it were only the sign!

Across from the bank in Wellington, you'll find **End of the Trail Antiques,** Paul and Margaret Fluesmeier's dandy collection of Native American tools, beadwork, and other artifacts. Don't worry if you're into other aspects of our past instead—there are plenty of other antiques as well, including baseball cards. Hours are Tuesday through Saturday 10:00 A.M. to 5:00 P.M. and Sunday 1:00 to 5:00 P.M. or call (816) 934–2544. Lovers of vintage clothing will find **Gingerbread House Antiques** (816–934–2712) fascinating; four really big, really loud dogs act as burglar alarms, but they're pussycats once you settle in to browse.

On the way into Lexington, watch for colorful sights guaranteed to make you smile, like the A-frame wedding chapel overlooking the river, the old Peckerwood Club, and a grain silo painted up to look like a lighthouse—and that glorious old river.

Once you enter historic Lexington, soak up the antebellum ambience. The homes along Highway 24 and on South Street are wonderful examples of Victorian charm—and, remember, we're not just talking 1890s gingerbread here. The Victorian era began in the 1840s. You'll itch to get inside some of these beauties; check with the Chamber of Commerce for dates and times on historic homes tours.

The area around the courthouse has plenty of places to browse. **Apple Creek Antiques and Gifts** is at 913 Main; across the street is the Rivertown Antiques Mall. **Ma & Pa's Bakin' Place** (816–259–6612) is a little farther down the block at 929 Main. This place is full of cookies, cakes, potato and salt-rising bread, and other freshly baked treats, and it opens at 6:00 A.M. every day except Sunday, so you can stop in before you hit the road. James Covey and the aptly named Karen Baker are the owners; these game young people have been known to attend local fairs in period costume, baking their delights outdoors in an old-fashioned woodstove.

Be sure to stop by the restored **Log House Museum** at 307 Broadway. This 1830s home was discovered in rundown condition and was moved and rebuilt log by log by the volunteer efforts of local citizens. Now it is surrounded by wildflowers and paths as it might have been when it was new. Spinning wheels, quilts, and other items of the era fill the little cabin, and a gift shop is in the back; admission is $2.00 for adults and $1.00 for children under twelve. Hours are Wednesday through Saturday 11:00 A.M. to 4:00 P.M. and Sunday noon to 4:00 P.M., but from November to April the house is open by appointment—it's too expensive to keep it warm through the winter months on a day-to-day basis. Call the log house at (816) 259–4711 during open hours, or call Mary Lou Edwards at (816) 259–6375 to book group or school tours any time (yes, even in winter, and even for individuals; Mary Lou will open up for you). She's also a fount of information about the home; she says they know everyone who ever lived there except the first owner.

The Battle of Lexington was fought in September 1861 when General Sterling Price moved his Confederate troops north after the Battle of Wilson's Creek and the fall of Springfield. After fifty-two hours of fighting, Union troops surrendered to the invaders. General Price took 3,000 prisoners and broke the chain of Union-held posts along the Missouri River. Remnants of the battle endure; a cannonball remains lodged in a pillar of the courthouse. You can still find earthworks out behind ⊃**Anderson House State Historic Site** (816–259–2112) overlooking the Missouri River. This red-brick house served as headquarters and hospital for both sides and is now a Civil War museum.

If you want to enmesh yourself in the era, Lexington is also the home of the **Graystone Bed and Breakfast,** owned by Cathy and Steve Lillard, at 324 Twenty-fifth Street (816–259–3476). It is an 1833 Greek Revival mansion on four tree-covered acres; all rooms have 1850s decor. Rates are $55 to $65 and include a continental breakfast.

Along Highway 24 toward Waverly, the land undergoes a change from fenced, row-cropped fields to orchards. The peach crop is always at risk in Missouri's unpredictable weather. Blossoms are often teased out early by a mild February to be punished by an April freeze. It is a dangerous business, but the area around Waverly perseveres. The best peaches from this area are huge and sweet and dripping with juice. A bad year for the peach business is when the fruit is too big, too juicy, and not nearly plentiful enough to make shipping profitable. This is bad for orchard owners but wonderful for anyone lucky enough to be driving through.

Highway 24 is the old Lewis and Clark Trail along the river. Now it is filled with markets where orchard owners sell their bounty to travelers. Pick up peaches and apples—or honey, homemade sausages, cheese, and cider—along this scenic drive.

The **Maharishi Kansas City Capital of the Age of Enlightenment,** believe it or not, is on Highway 24 near Waverly. There Rob and Joanne Anibal manage an elegant 75-room residence-course facility on 260 forested acres, covered with walking trails, wildlife, and a fountain. The house can be home to as many as forty-five people, mostly businesspeople, doctors, and lawyers from the Kansas City area who practice transcendental meditation, or TM (there are over a thousand on the mailing list; as many as 5,000 people who practice TM in the Kansas City area). The clinic is a Maharishi Ayur-Veda health education center where you can check in for five days and learn the discipline of TM, and enjoy the oil massage and herbal spa baths for a profound state of rest. Ann Hays (816–491–9161) is the person to call to make reservations for the week. The cost of a room, with gourmet vegetarian meals, is only $25 a day. The TM classes are on a sliding scale based on ability to pay; the average for a businessperson is about $400. There is a free lifetime follow-up program at the center in Kansas City as well.

For those of you already practicing TM, the center offers two- and three-day weekends of rejuvenation therapy (an hour-and-a-half oil massage, steam baths, herbal spa) so you can get your body, mind, and spirit back in balance after a tough week. The cost is $120 for two days, $160 for three days, complete with vegetarian meals. Each room has its own mood and is uniquely decorated. If you would just like to tour the facility when you are passing through Waverly, call ahead at (816) 493–2285; they will be happy to open the gates and take you on a tour inside the magnificent estate with its three gold domes, all built by volunteers with donated money. To find the center go west on Highway 24 from Waverly about 6 miles to Burkhart Orchards. Across the street from the orchards is a drive leading to the center (about a half mile back).

The land along Highway 65 outside Marshall reveals the real beauty of a productive agricultural landscape—mile after mile of substantial farm buildings crisply painted and in good repair. Huge silos and solid fencing speak of people who care about the land and whose care has paid off. Fields of corn, milo, soybeans, and wheat change color with the seasons and reflect more than 150 years of farming here. In the spring, Missouri farmland is at its most beautiful.

While in Marshall you will see several intriguing Victorian homes along Business Route 65 that are now antiques and gift shops. The town of Marshall is typical of the best of small-town America. It's the county seat of Saline County; the red-brick courthouse in the center of the square boasts a tall, domed turret with a clock tower.

About a mile outside the town of ⊃**Arrow Rock** on Highway 41 stands a comfortable white Victorian house shaded by old trees. It is now the home of Bob and Chris Rappold's Evergreen Restaurant (816–837–3251), a good spot to have a quiet dinner during the season at Arrow Rock's Lyceum Theater. Warm antiques and a fireplace in every room create a cozy ambience in which to enjoy really fine country cooking. Chris's Chocolate Mousse Cake is a sinful way to finish a meal; if you want to feel more virtuous, order the seasonal fruit tart. Evergreen closes after Christmas and opens again in the spring.

Bob and Chris are new owners of the Evergreen; they were proprietors of Cafe Europa in Columbia. If it's any indication of how good their food is, former happy customers drive all the way from Columbia to find them at their new location, where they've kept some of the old Evergreen's recipes while adding favorites from Cafe Europa.

During the theater season, hours for lunch are 11:30 A.M. to 3:00 P.M., 5:30 to 8:30 P.M. for dinner, open Sundays from 4:00 to

7:00 P.M.; in the winter Evergreen is open Friday, Saturday, and Sunday. If you have a group and let Bob know ahead of time, they'll open *any* time for private parties. Historical gossip is that Jesse James once hid upstairs; listen quietly and you may hear his ghost.

Pioneers stopped at historic Arrow Rock on their way west; it was a Santa Fe Trail town, a river port, and a meeting place for those who shaped history. More than forty original buildings remain. Arrow Rock is a real town, with permanent residents, a grocery store, a gas station, and a post office, but it is also a state park and historic site. The state leases out the Old Tavern Inn; dinners are bounteous and amazingly inexpensive ($9.95 will buy a huge meal, from salad to dessert). The museum is upstairs.

Arrow Rock looks like a normal town—normal for a hundred years ago, that is. Streets and gutters are made from huge blocks of limestone; board sidewalks clatter with footsteps. The old bank acts as ticket office for the Lyceum, and the tiny stone jail still waits for an inmate. You may camp at Arrow Rock State Park; sites are available for groups or individuals.

Today, the **Lyceum Repertory Theatre** (816–837–3311) offers performances throughout the summer in an old church building; it's Missouri's oldest repertory company. Call ahead for a list of plays and their rotating dates.

If you've found the Lyceum just off the main street, you've found Wanda Summerstar Duren's and Two Dogs Pasola's place, as well—the **Summerstar and Two Dogs Trading Post** (816–837–3408). Chuck Duren makes beautiful handmade knives with antler handles—some as they come from the animal, others with intricate carvings.

Borgman's Bed and Breakfast (816–837–3350) is a nine-teenth-century inn with five bedrooms and a common game room. Play a quick round of Scrabble, or enjoy a fireside chat with the Borgmans. Mother and daughter team Helen and Kathy Borgman did much of the restoration work themselves; take a look at the fascinating "house book," which shows step-by-step what's been done. Helen will fix you a generous breakfast, and Kathy will give you a tour of the town—she's an official Arrow Rock guide. Additional meals are available if you make prior arrangements. A cat and bird are in residence, so no other pets are welcomed. Rates are $40 for a double. (Next door to Borgman's is Keelor Handweaving, where you can buy yourself a warm, luxurious treat.)

Artist George Caleb Bingham's home is here (remember him from Independence?), as is the home of Dr. John Sappington, one of the first to use quinine to treat malaria; Kathy Borgman will tell you all about it.

One and a half miles west of Arrow Rock on Highway TT Chuck and Jeanie Holland have a restored antebellum country home with three rooms furnished in period antiques (one downstairs with private bath) waiting for you at the **Airey Hill Bed and Breakfast.** A full country breakfast of ham and eggs, quiche with homemade muffins, or pancakes greets you each morning. Rooms have double beds and are $45 a night. The home is "out in the country" according to Jeanie, so call (816) 886–5815 for reservations.

At **Boonville,** following the river east, the western prairie meets the Ozarks. The town was settled in 1810 by the widow Hannah Cole, who, with her nine children, built cabins on the bluffs overlooking the Missouri River. During the War of 1812 the settlement was palisaded and named Cole's Fort. It became the main river port for all of southwestern Missouri.

The older residential section of Boonville has an unusually well preserved collection of antebellum brick residences with wide halls and large rooms. Modest neoclassical homes are mixed with more flamboyant Victorian ones; many are on the National Register of Historic Places.

While in Boonville visit the **Old Cooper County Jail and Hanging Barn** at 614 East Morgan. The jail was built in 1848 and used until 1978 when public hanging was declared cruel and unusual punishment. Prisoners' quarters resemble dungeons, where the inmates were sometimes shackled to the wall with metal rings. Outside the jail is the hanging barn where nineteen-year-old Lawrence Mabry was executed in 1930, the state's last public hanging (as told in historian Bob Dyer's folk song, "The Last Man to Hang in Missouri").

‡**Thespian Hall** is the oldest theater still in use west of the Alleghenies. Originally built in 1857, it has been used as an army barracks, Civil War hospital, and skating rink, among other things. It has featured gymnastics, opera, and movies in its day and is now the home of the Boonville Community Theatre.

If you are out walking around, search out Harley Park, where Lookout Point sits atop a bluff over the Missouri River, and get a feel for what early townsfolk saw along the long bend of the river. An Indian burial mound surmounts this high point; imagine the prospect of immortality with such a view.

The mid-Missouri area was the site of many of the key battles of the Civil War. The first land battle of the war was fought 4 miles below Boonville on June 17, 1861. State troops under the command of Confederate Colonel John S. Marmaduke were defeated by federal forces led by Captain Nathaniel Lyon. Military historians consider this victory important in preserving the Union.

Jefferson City, Missouri's capital, is smack in the center of the state on Highway 50, handy to legislators and lobbyists. Built on the steep southern bluffs of the Missouri, the city and the surrounding rural landscape offer considerable scenic variety. Large streams are bordered with steeply sloping and heavily forested hills. Bottomland here is rich with alluvial and yellow loess soils that don't look the way you expect fertile topsoil to look but support more wheat and corn than any other section of the Ozarks.

Here also is one of the last of the riverfront landings—ↃJefferson Landing, one of the busiest centers of the nineteenth century. It's still busy; the Amtrak station is at the landing, as are the Lohman Building, the Union Hotel, and the Maus House.

Christopher Maus House was built in 1854, a fine example of the small, red-brick residences built in Jefferson City during the mid-nineteenth century. The Elizabeth Rozier Gallery and the Missouri State Art Museum are located here, with shows throughout the year.

The Executive Mansion is just east of Jefferson Landing. Reservations are necessary to tour it (call 314–751–4141), but you can enjoy the magnificent grounds at any time.

The State Capitol is certainly *on* the path; however, once inside the House Lounge, you will find a mural painted in 1935 by Thomas Hart Benton. This mural stirred controversy in 1936—some of the legislators said it lacked refinement. Always quick with an answer, Benton retorted that he portrayed "people involved in their natural, daily activities that did not require being polite."

Locals indoctrinate out-of-state relatives and visitors at **Arris's Pizza,** 117 West High Street (314–635–9225). It's a must. Owner Arris Pardalos now has a small chain of restaurants where the gyros have a very special flavor. Hours are 11:00 A.M. to midnight Monday through Thursday and until 2:00 A.M. on Friday and Saturday, noon until 11:00 P.M. on Sunday.

Missouri's Melting Pot

Head west to California (that's California, Missouri) on Highway 50 and ⊃**Burgers' Smokehouse** if you fancy a ham to carry home. It is open from 7:30 A.M. to 5:00 P.M. (314–796–3134), 3 miles south of California on Highway 87 (just follow the signs). This family-owned smokehouse has been in business for the past twenty-five years and is one of the largest country meat-processing plants in the United States, producing 200,000 hams annually.

What you wouldn't expect to find here are the seasonal dioramas, which show the beauty of the Ozarks with great care for botanical and zoological detail. These scenes by artist Terry Chase depict the influence of Ozark geography and changing seasons on the process of curing meat.

If you feel in the gallery mood—or just in the mood for a fascinating chat with a man who always has time to sit down and have a cup of coffee—check out Beryl White's studio and gallery at 401 North High Street (314–796–2303). Beryl has been restoring this old Victorian storefront building for some time; it is now on the National Register. It's just the place if you're running short of sketching supplies while dawdling off the path. Beryl stocks everything from books to brushes and offers oil-painting classes as well.

Memory Lane Bed and Breakfast is also in California. This 1896 Victorian is filled with antiques and is next door to an antiques shop, too. The three guest rooms have double beds and twin beds and all share a hall bath. The room rate of $35 includes a hearty breakfast. Call Ozark Mountain Country Reservation Service at (800) 695–1546 for more information.

Highway 50 will take you to the town of Tipton. Follow the signs to the ⊃**Dutch Bakery and Bulk Food Store** (816–433–2865). Located on Highways 5 and 50 at the west end of Tipton, the shop is owned by Leonard and Suetta Hoover. Suetta does all the baking right here in the house while minding their six children and seems unruffled by it all. Old Order Mennonites, they came here from Pennsylvania and speak Pennsylvania Dutch when alone in the shop or talking to the kids. Her pies are baked from home-grown berries and fruit; fresh vegetables from their garden are available in season. Homemade breads (a favorite is a wonderful oatmeal bread) and rolls fill shelves along with bulk foods. But the primary reason for stopping here is the

"Dutch letters"—crisp, thick pastry rolled and filled with almond paste and shaped into letters. They are cheaper if you buy five, and you might as well so you won't have to turn around and come back in an hour.

At the intersection of Highway 50 and Highway 65 in Sedalia is an old-fashioned fifties drive-in called the **Wheel Inn.** Carhops will serve you, or go inside; either way, you must try their famous Guberburger—a hamburger grilled with peanut butter and served with mayonnaise, tomato, lettuce, and pickles. Before you shout "Yuck!" try it. They are deadly good and habit forming. Note: The Wheel Inn is closed on Tuesdays.

Or if you're in the mood for some really good barbecue, turn south on Highway 65 at that intersection and drive to 1915 South Limit to **Kehde's Barbecue** (816–826–2267), where John and Chelsea Kehde (pronounced K.D.) serve the best barbecue in the area. But that's not all, Kehde's also has jalapeño fries (french fries dipped in some kind of spicy coating) and a *grilled* tenderloin sandwich that is as good as the fried kind but without all the fat. Kehde's is a regular stop for folks headed to or from the Lake of the Ozarks and Kansas City.

If you drive into Sedalia on Highway 65, you will probably pass (off to your left and way up) a beautiful stone mansion overlooking the highway. It is Stony-ridge Farm in ⊃**Bothwell State Park.** Bothwell chose limestone as his primary building material for the lodge and cliff house. There are more angles to this place than a Chinese puzzle—it must have driven the roofers crazy. The original carriage road rises almost 100 feet but in a gentle ascent, with the lay of the land; hand-laid stone culverts allow water passage under the road. Take the first left after you pass the house on Highway 65 going toward Sedalia (or, driving north, watch very carefully for the small sign marking the turn, or you will have to turn around and go back when you finally see it). It is worth the trouble to find; there are spectacular views and wonderful walking trails near the house.

Also in Sedalia is the **Sedalia House** (816–826–6615). Innkeepers Dan and Brenda Ice welcome guests to their lovely, two-story colonial home, which is elegantly furnished. The surrounding countryside is beautiful year round. This is a 300-acre working farm that includes a creek and woods. Deer and turkey hunting are available in season, and rooms include a full breakfast. Rates are $48 and up—$55 with private bath.

Bothwell State Park

There are several antiques malls in Sedalia, but remember that in August this is the home of the Missouri State Fair, which brings in over 300,000 people. The path gets beaten smooth, but it leads to midway rides, big-name entertainment, livestock shows, and car races—good, clean, all-American fun.

Don't leave Sedalia without finding the **Town and Country Shoe Factory and Outlet** on Highway 50 on the west edge of town, where they sell quality shoes at bargain prices. (If the shoe fits, buy it.)

If you continue west on Interstate 70, you will come to the town of Odessa and be in for an old-fashioned treat, because that is where the **Odessa Ice Cream Factory** can be found. Owners Marty Beamer and Steve Barker make Odessa Ice Cream and Holy Cow Honey Ice Cream a few feet from where customers walk up and buy it. The shop has been there since 1928, making ice cream in the same room with most of the vintage equipment, turning out an average of 300 gallons of ice cream a week during the summer. The two young men bought the factory a few years ago and have spent time and money renovating the retail shop. The factory also makes things like chocolate sauce and popcorn, but, because it is a small business fighting the competition of the big guys, it prides itself on being the friendliest as well as turning out the richest, finest, old-fashioned ice cream to be found anywhere. There is no "lite" anything and no yogurt. But what the heck, go for it! How often do you get to Odessa anyway?

Western Missouri waited a long time for a botanical garden; St. Louis, on the east, has one of the finest in the country. Finally, after much hemming and hawing among folks in the Greater Kansas City area and those just over the Kansas border, the people of ⊃**Powell Gardens** couldn't wait any longer and began their own. Hurrah for private initiative! This is a beautiful, not-for-profit, 807-acre garden and natural resource center where you can wander among the flowers and indigenous plants, learn about "S-s-s-s-snakes!," make an all-natural wreath, or learn how to plant, prune, and harvest your own backyard botanical garden— you get the idea. Hours are Tuesday to Friday from 8:00 A.M. to 5:00 P.M. and weekends from 9:00 A.M. to 6:00 P.M. Powell Gardens (816–566–2600) is just south of Highway 50 at Kingsville.

Watch for signs from Interstate 70 (or Highway 291) for Fleming Park and Lake Jacomo. You'll find the usual sailing, swimming, and fishing as well as the Burroughs Audubon Society Library (816–795–8177). Learn about the birds, take a hike, browse through the books, and discover how to turn your backyard into a wildlife sanctuary. The library is open from noon to 4:30 P.M.

Stop in your tracks. The world is moving altogether too quickly, but there's an antidote: ⊃**Missouri Town 1855** in Fleming Park. Managed by the Jackson County Parks Department, one of the two largest county parks departments in the United States, it's a collection of original mid-nineteenth-century buildings moved on site. They now make up a brand-new old town founded in 1960.

A wide variety of architectural styles add to the historical significance of the town. It's just that sort of progression from rugged log cabins to fine homes that would have taken place in the last century as settlers arrived and commerce thrived. You'll find antebellum homes, a tavern, a schoolhouse, a church, a lawyer's tiny office (apparently the law was not quite so lucrative then), and the mercantile, where settlers would have bought outright or bartered for their goods. It has even been the setting for several movies, including the television version of *Friendly Per-*

suasion, and the more recent movie *Across Five Aprils,* a story of a family split by the Civil War.

If the buildings alone aren't enough to pique your interest, this is a "living history" experience. You're liable to see the blacksmith at work, watch oxen tilling the soil, or be followed by the resident flock of geese. You can wander around a real herb garden and discover how many were used as medicinals in the past century—hospitals were rare in those days, and medical insurance was unheard of.

Missouri Town 1855 is on the east side of Fleming Park. Take Colbern Road east to Cyclone School Road. Turn north (left) and follow the signs two miles to the entrance. Admission for adults is $3.00, youths are $1.00 and children under four are free. The town is open Wednesday through Sunday from 9:00 A.M. till 5:00 P.M. from April 15 through November 15 and on weekends only from November till April.

Lee's Summit is worth a drive through if you are "antiquing" in the area; this collection of towns is full of antiques malls and shops. American Heritage Mall at 220 South Douglas and Lee's Summit Antiques Mall at Third Street and Highway 50 are worth a stop.

◌**Unity Village,** on Highway 50 just west of Lee's Summit, is an incorporated town with its own post office and government. It's a peaceful setting with an old-world feel; spacious grounds contain a natural rock bridge, Spanish Mediterranean–style buildings, and a formal rose garden with reflecting pools and fountains. People of all faiths use the resources at Unity. The restaurant, bookstore, and chapel are open to the public, and you may arrange an overnight stay by calling (816) 524–3550.

Little Greenwood is just south of Lee's Summit on Highway 291, then east on Highway 150. This was once a bustling place with not one but two train stations—a major shipping locus for cattle and lumber. It still has two explosives factories and a rock quarry nearby, accounting for the heavy trucks rumbling through this sleepy town.

An old wooden bridge marks the end of downtown proper; watch for signs to find any number of little antiques stores and factory outlets. ◌**Greenwood Antiques and Tea Room** is a mall-type operation hard by the railroad bridge and just full of small booths. The food is excellent; add your name to the waiting list when you go in the door, and they'll find you.

This book can't begin to list all of the antiques shops, tea rooms, and outlet stores in this town. But one of the newest and most beautiful is Claire Fellows's **Country Charm Antique and Craft Mall** one block south of Highway 150 on Allendale Lake Road. Here two floors of primitives, handmade country clothing, collectibles, and antiques share space with a country tea room where Claire makes the daily specials and pies. The chalkboard lists dishes such as mushroom or tomato pie and popovers all made from old recipes found in cookbooks she collects. Try the fruit cream pie with the seasonal fruit—the blueberry cream is particularly delicious—and enjoy the frontier banjo music playing softly in the background. Hours are Tuesday through Saturday 10:00 A.M. to 5:00 P.M., Sunday from noon until 5:00 P.M. You can get a list of all of the antiques shops in Greenwood at your first stop and spend the day checking them out.

Before you skip town, stop in at **Henderson and Park** (816–537–6388) at Seventeenth Street and Highway 150. Dinah Henderson will answer questions about wildlife, gardening, fishing, or wool gathering. She and a friend shear sheep, card wool, and make some of the warmest and loveliest garments you'll ever see, right here in the store.

Civil War buffs will discover facts about a number of famous Missouri battles at the **Civil War Museum of Jackson County** in Lone Jack (816–881–4431). You'll find the battlefield marked for self-guided tours; there's also a cemetery and Civil War artifacts on display.

The museum is located just past the intersection of Highway 50 and Highway 150; admission fees are the same as for Missouri Town 1855. Summer hours are the same as well, but the museum is open from November 15 to April 15 by appointment only.

If you still haven't gotten enough of the War between the States, head south and east of Warrensburg to **Cedarcroft Farm** at 431 Southeast Y Highway, where Bill and Sandra Wayne have an 1867 farmhouse on eighty scenic acres to share with you. Bill is a Civil War reenactor and historian who can tell you a lot about the history of this area. He belongs to a reenactment unit based in Warrensburg that makes living history presentations, joins parades, and works at historic sites. He even has a uniform you can try on and a musket he will teach you to shoot. Sandra turns out a "more-than-you-can-eat" country breakfast accompanied by cookies, fudge, nut bread, and a table full of country cooking. The two guest rooms are decorated with period furniture. The house was built by Sandra's great grandfather who was a Union soldier. Rooms are $45 for two (with room for four at $12.50 each extra). They will even pick you up at the Amtrak station. Call (816) 747–5728.

Warrensburg is the home of Central Missouri State University. It is a fair-to-middlin'-size city now as it grows with the university. Coming into town on Highway 13 or Highway 50, you may have noticed several life-size animal sculptures made of scrap metal or pieces of wood. These are the handiwork of sculptor Jim Myers. Jim says he has been making scrap-wood sculptures since he was a kid; his dad owned a lumber yard. He studied at the Hollywood Art Center in California and the Paris American Academy in France before returning to open his ⊃**Contemporary Gallerie** (816–429–2107) in 1982, where he displays his smaller wood sculptures and oils.

The **Camel Crossing Bed and Breakfast** at 210 East Gay (816–429–2973) belongs to Joyce and Ed Barnes. It is a lovely turn-of-the-century home in the residential area near the university. Tastefully decorated with Middle Eastern and Oriental

Jim Myers Sculpture

93

accents gathered while the couple lived in Saudi Arabia, the place has a unique flavor, including a collection of several hundred camel figures. A camel crossing sign is used as their logo. Rates are $47, or $57 with private bath.

If you are headed north on Highway 13, there is a little surprise waiting for you about 4 miles north of Warrensburg near Fayetteville. Standing patiently near the highway are Ogbid and his wife Ishtar watching traffic roll by day after day. Ogbid and Ishtar are made of old oil drums, engine pistons, metal buckets, and assorted springs and reflectors, giving them a nightlife of sorts. Their son Nimrod joined them a few years ago. Nimrod resembles his parents, although he is unique in that his head is an old metal chamber pot.

Just recently Cousin It joined the family. He is made from an old water heater with a freon canister for a head, and he's covered with thousands of yards of baling wire, each strand individually attached. Cousin It, with 150 pounds of hair, looks more like a furry family pet than a relative. The creator, J. C. Carter, lives up the hill. He's had fun with his hobby of creating "assembled metal sculptures," sort of recycling-gone-bonkers. He has visions when he sees industrial junk—freon canisters and chamber pots take on a life of their own. But he pulls the whole community into the fun. When locals complained that Ishtar and Ogbid looked lonely standing out there, he threw a wedding complete with preacher, cake, reception, and bird seed to throw (instead of rice) there at the corner, then carted the 1,400-pound wedding couple off for their honeymoon. A couple of weeks later they returned with Nimrod. (Gestation period of robots is sort of undetermined at this time.) Cousin It will soon be joined by "The Reaper," and Carter has opened a place where all of his creations can be displayed. Call Carter at (816) 747–5506 to see his other works.

Bristle Ridge Winery, between Warrensburg and Knob Noster, is ½ mile south of Highway 50 at Montserrat and produces quality wines that range from subtle dry whites to bright sweet reds. It sits on a hill with a panoramic view, the perfect spot to picnic with a bottle of wine, bread, cheese, and summer sausage—all sold at Bristle Ridge. Open Saturdays 10:00 A.M. to 5:00 P.M. and Sunday noon until 5:00 P.M. Closed January, February, and holidays (816–229–0961).

The Ozarks

Cole Camp is a tiny town that would be easy to miss, but don't. The first place to stop, if you have planned this right and it is lunchtime, is ⊃**Der Essen Platz** (816–668–3080). It's on the corner—you can't miss it, the town is small—and it's open seven days a week. Owners Larry and Ronda Shackelford's German-style restaurant features imported beers and food and a Friday buffet from 5:00 P.M. to 9:00 P.M., April through December. Cream pies of a variety not found elsewhere (unless you come from a German neighborhood) are a specialty; try German chocolate pie with coconut, or lemon pie with sour cream, crumb topping, and whipped cream. Joyce Schlesselmann, dining room manager, brought out samples of the wurst sandwiches (a pun—laugh, don't groan!) they offer. The menu includes *kasseler rippchen* (smoked boneless pork chops served on sauerkraut), sauerbraten (marinated beef on a bed of spatzle and gingersnap gravy), and if you are a schnitzel fan, *schweineschnitzel, wiener schnitzel,* and *jaeger schnitzel.*

Now waddle out of "the eating place" and turn right to **Melville's Antiques and Restoration,** 108 South Maple (816– 826–6570). Owner Rory Melville will take you on a tour of his sawdust-covered workshop, where he specializes in the restoration of antiques. Detail work includes brass and copper polishing, chair caning, and veneer repair. Melville also has three buildings full of antiques that look like they did when great-grandmother first bought them. Specializing in top quality golden oak and Victorian walnut furniture, he also has a large assortment of turn-of-the-century brass lighting fixtures and offers expert antique lamp restoration.

Pick up a copy of the Antiques and Shop Guide and stroll around town. You will find many, many places to poke around.

While you are in Cole Camp, stop by Jim Maxwell's shop, right around the corner from Der Essen Platz, and take a look at his caricature woodcarvings. The finely detailed carvings feature Missouri coal miners, gangsters, artillery men from the Civil War, and doughboys of World War I. The limited edition carvings are original pieces of art sought after by collectors. Maxwell is the author of two woodcarving books and creates a variety of subjects from casually styled Ozark Hill people to very accurately detailed caricatures of other bygone eras.

About 3 miles east of Cole Camp on Highway 52 is a pretty little shop sitting alone by the side of the road. It's **Calico Country Cupboard** (816–668–4896), where owner Sally Howell features country clocks as well as quilts and gifts, all handmade. Hours are 10:00 A.M. to 5:00 P.M. daily, and Sunday noon to 6:00 P.M. (closed Tuesday). Winter hours will vary.

Take a left (north) on Highway 152 between Cole Camp and Stover and drive to Highway M. Right there at the intersection you will find **Orland Pennel's Craft Shop.** Orland will custom make any kind of swing, lounge chair, birdhouse, or glider in his woodwork shop there in the shed by his house. He also has some items all ready to load up and take away stacked in a gazebo in the yard. Call (314) 377–4770 to be sure he is home; he doesn't keep any regular hours, and that's just the way he wants it.

Highway 52 runs into Highway 5 at the city of Versailles (pronounced just as it looks, not the French way). Versailles is the gateway to the Lake of the Ozarks area. Here you make the decision to go east on Highway 52 to the St. Louis side of the lake or southwest on Highway 5 to the Kansas City side. But before you decide anything, drive to the square and check out **Omi's Apple Haus,** 100 North Fisher (314–378–5491). It opened in the fall of 1989. Jerry and Gesila Highland are the owners; sister-in-law Connie Highland manages it. Omi's (German for "grandma") sells handmade items from local Mennonites: quilts, mincemeat, honey, dolls, and dresses and bonnets for little girls. At Omi's you can pick up a brochure listing the other shops in town.

The Lake of the Ozarks area is called the "Land of the Magic Dragon." If you look at the lake on a map and go snake-eyed, it has a dragon shape; hence the name. The Ozark heritage stems from the first immigrants here who were from Tennessee, Kentucky, and nearby parts of the southern Appalachians. The Upper-South hill-country folks were descended from Scottish-Irish stock.

For many years the Ozark Mountains sheltered these folks and few outsiders entered the area; you may have heard of the Irish Wilderness. Because of the rough topography, the railroads avoided the area, and this extreme isolation until about fifty years ago created the "Ozark Hillbilly." The values, lifestyle, and beliefs of those first settlers are still much in evidence.

The building of Bagnell Dam to form the Lake of the Ozarks eroded that isolation and turned the area into the Midwest's summer playground. Because it is not a Corps of Engineers lake, homes can be built right on the water's edge; the 1,300 miles of serpentine shore is more shoreline than the state of California has!

Miles of lake coves, wooded hills, and steep dusty roads are still unsettled. Most undeveloped areas have no roads at all leading to them. The east side of the lake, which houses the dam, has become the drop-in tourist side. The track is beaten slick over here. There are restaurants, shopping malls, and water slides galore.

Some of the unique places on the east side deserve a mention before you head to the west side of the lake, where the more fascinating spots hide. If you go to Bagnell Dam from Eldon, watch for wintering eagles—here and at most of the lake crossings. They retreat from the Arctic chill up north, following flocks of migrating geese.

You may not have thought of Missouri as a big state for bald eagle watching—and spring through early fall, it's not, though a captive breeding program of the Missouri Department of Conservation has been in effect since 1981 to reestablish a wild breeding population. But come winter, these big birds take up residence wherever they can find open water and plentiful feeding. One recent year, over 1,400 bald eagles were counted, making this state second only to Washington in the lower forty-eight states for eagle sightings. At most Missouri lakes, their main diet consists of fish—they have far better luck with fishing than most humans.

Taking the back way around the lake along Highway 52 to Eldon and then Highway 54 to Bagnell Dam is more interesting than the much-traveled and very crowded Highway 5–54 route.

A left turn (north) on Highway 5 puts you in the middle of the Mennonite community. On the roads around Versailles, horse-drawn buggies carry Mennonite citizens on their daily tasks. They are less strict than the Jamesport Amish—the somber black attire is uncommon—and most of the homes have telephones and electricity, though many don't. Old Order Mennonite women wear prayer bonnets but dress in printed fabrics. Some families have cars, but many of the cars are painted black—chrome and all. To get a good tour of the area, begin on Highway 5 at Versailles and follow it to a sign announcing the turnoff for Lehmans' if you plan to be in the area for a couple of days.

↻**Lehmans'** (816–337–6272) is a couple of miles off Highway 5 on Route 2 (watch for the sign). This is a no-so-well-kept secret and popular with the locals, but tourists are unaware of it, for the most part. Mennonites Carl and Anna Mary Lehman and their daughter Barbara welcome you to this private home about 1½ miles off Highway 5. Another daughter, Ginny, serves guests and makes the fine quilts for sale here.

There are fresh vegetables in season, this morning's eggs from the barn, and frozen homemade jam and vegetables in winter. Bring wine or beer if you want to, but no hard liquor. They serve two kinds of pie with the meal, and when the season is right, fresh strawberry and peach pie or cobbler. Choose the meat when making a reservation—smoked turkey, ham, beef, or chicken—and they do the rest. The three-course dinner includes six salads, two veggies, homemade rolls, and dessert, and takes about one and a half hours; don't be in a hurry. They can seat as few as six or as many as forty using several rooms in the house. You must call twelve to twenty-four hours in advance.

Highway 5 passes through the tiny berg of Fortuna. This is a seriously small town. Just past the post office you will see ↻**Kurtz General Store,** often with a horse and buggy tied out front (816–337–6267). Architectural interest is not the store's strong point, but longevity is: This simple white shop has been in business since 1902, selling hand-carved toys, quilts, and homemade noodles as well as general merchandise. It is owned by Ruth and Melvin Kurtz, Mennonites who take pride in the store's heritage.

Backtrack a little to where Highway 5 splits into Highway 52 and follow Highway 52 east to Highway C on the left. Stay on Highway C about 4 miles east of Highway 52 and, in the summertime, watch for **Zimmerman's Market** on the left. The Zimmermans are a Mennonite family who have a garden that covers acres of land and is worked by hand by the family. The little shop there has fresh produce to match the season, and it carries fresh milk, butter, and homemade breads, along with cheeses from other Mennonite farms in the area. Homemade noodles, sorghum molasses, honey, jelly, and fresh eggs also fill the little shop. You can call (314) 378–4836 to see what's available today.

Follow Highway C about 6 miles to ↻**Pleasant Valley Quilts and Tea Room** (there is a sign by the road where you can turn and drive about three quarters of a mile on gravel). The Brubaker

Kurtz General Store

family gathers a fine selection of quilts and crafts from Mennonite families in the area. Their daughters Lydia and Lucille handle the quilt shop, where quilts of all sizes and colors are hung for display. In fact, quilts will be made to order for you if you have a particular color or style in mind. Quilts made by local Mennonite ladies join aprons, dolls, and other hand-crafted items for sale here. Daughter Marian has the tea shop, where daily special sandwiches are written on the chalkboard by the door. Call (314) 378–6151. They are open from 8:00 A.M. to 5:00 P.M. every day but Sunday.

Turn north on Highway E, then follow E to Highway K (this sounds harder than it really is), but watch closely for horse-drawn buggies and bicycles on these hilly back roads. Highway K leads east to the tiny, tiny town of Excelsior and **Weavers' Market,** serving this community of about 250 Mennonite families. Weavers' carries fresh-frozen farm produce, frozen home-made pies ready to pop into your oven, an enormous assortment of teas and spices, and other bulk foods, including homemade noodles. Nearby (follow the signs) is **Excelsior Fabric,** where

Anna and Sam Shirk and their family carry an extensive collection of quilting fabrics.

If you turn left back at Highway E on a Sunday morning about 10:00 A.M., you will come to the Clearview Mennonite Church and see dozens of horse-drawn buggies tied up in stables and at hitching posts around the church. It's quite a sight.

Also on Highway E between that church and the Bethel Mennonite Church, the Martin family offers fine home-cooked meals. Look sharp for the house, for there is only a martin house in the front yard (with a sign on it saying **Martin House**) and no other signs. Pull around to the back entrance; the restaurant is on the lower level. Anna and Harvey Martin turn out Pennsylvania Dutch meals, and you select the menu from meat through dessert. Choose from roast beef, chicken, ham, and pork ribs. There is also ham or beef meatloaf. The vegetable and salad come from the Martin garden (the fruit salad is full of fresh apples and covered with an orange sauce), the rolls are, of course, homemade, and the pies are whatever kind of fruit or cream pie you choose. This meal is only $8.00 a person, with a six-person minimum. (One dollar extra gets you a second meat, $2.00 a third.) You must call twenty-four hours in advance to reserve a table, and the Martins can seat slightly more than fifty people. You may bring a bottle of wine to enjoy with your meal, if you wish. Call (314) 378–4578 for reservations.

Now find your way back to Highway 52 and take a left (east) to Leah Zimmerman's bake shop (a sign on the highway says FARMER'S MARKET). Leah's is the first house on the left; a large sign in her yard says **Shady Oak Market.** Her buggy is near the barn, where her horse Jessica waits for excursions to the grocery store, Weavers' market, or church on Sunday. Leah has produce from her own wonderful garden, but she also is the source for eggs from free-range chickens, fresh fruit from family orchards, and a whole range of baked goods she turns out daily. Cinnamon bread, pies with whatever fresh fruit is in season, cookies, jams, and canned goods deck her shelves in the pantry just off the front porch. The sign says COME IN and that's just what it means. She's usually in the kitchen baking something tasty—she does custom baking for regulars—and comes out when she hears the door slam. Call (314) 378–6401 to order something special (in the fall her apple dumplings are wonderful!).

Along the same route is a wonderfully old-fashioned bed and breakfast called **The Farm.** It is, indeed, a working farm with no pretensions (there are clothes hanging on the line and rusted tractor parts lying about); this place is neither quaint nor picturesque. Owners Gail and Larry Schmitz offer an old-fashioned trip to grandma's. There is one double bed in the guest room, and the kids can camp out in a big tent. They can also fetch eggs, milk the cow or goat, and go for mule-drawn wagon rides on the back roads. Best times are spring and fall because there is no air-conditioning, and the room gets "a little chilly" in winter, according to Gail. Cooking is done on a wood-burning stove. Gail says you can have anything you want for breakfast, and for only $6.00 a plate you can join the family for dinner—roast goose, leg of lamb, or whatever she's cooking that night. Reservations must be made through River Country Bed and Breakfast (800–728–0721 or 314–771–1993).

The difference between the east and west sides of the lake has been described as like "flipping channels between 'Hee Haw' and 'Lifestyles of the Rich and Famous'." Welcome to the St. Louis side, a road more traveled but still lots of fun.

There's a must-stop spot on Highway 54 between Bagnell Dam and Camdenton at Osage Beach. The **Osage Village Mall** is an outdoor mall that features nothing but factory outlet stores. The place is huge, and if you are aware of name-brand prices elsewhere, you will go crazy here.

Highway 54 through Osage Beach is, in a word, touristy. The path here is not only beaten, it's three lanes wide and heavy with traffic in the summer—the bumper-to-bumper grid-lock type you came here to get away from. The road is filled to overflowing with craft shops, flea markets, bumper cars, and water slides. There are plenty of good eating places, from fast-food chains to little places like the **Wickerleigh's Porch,** where you can find a good-for-your-heart breakfast as early as 7:00 A.M. (and you can also find Eggs Benedict), and the **Peace-'n'-Plenty Country Cafe** in Poverty Flats Village (near State Road KK), specializing in homemade soups, sandwiches, breads, and salads.

Joe Orr is a Missouri artist who is gaining a well-deserved reputation. You can see why for yourself at his elegant new gallery/studio/home right next to TanTara on Highway KK in Osage Beach. The **Orr Gallery and Studio** also features Rita

101

Orr's wonderful silk-screens and monoprints. But that's not all that is tucked away in this second-floor hideaway. Displayed here are Ron Schroeder's sculptures, Paul Clervi's bronze sculptures, Steve Johnson's contemporary free-form pottery, and Rhonda Cearlock's raku pottery. Joe is the founder of the National Oil and Acrylic Painters Society, which has a national exhibition here in November with over 600 artists from thirty states entered for exhibit. Joe's and Rita's studios are on the gallery level of their home, too, and open if you want to watch them at work. Hours are from 10:00 A.M. until 5:00 P.M. daily, but Joe is quick to add that it's "sort of by chance or appointment, too," so calling ahead (314–348–2232) might be a good idea.

The **Potted Steer Restaurant** (314–348–5053) is in a comfortable-looking wooden building tucked in at the west end of the Grand Glaize Bridge on Highway 54 in Osage Beach. Owner Joseph Boer, a native of Holland who came to this country on refugee status on Christmas Day in 1956, opened the restaurant in 1971. It is a very laid-back place where casual clothes are the rule and long waits are expected. But the crowd is vacation-loose and fun. The specialty here is deep-fried lobster tail (which sounds like heresy to a seafood lover). Boer says he has never tasted the creation that made the restaurant famous. You see, he hates seafood.

To tide you over until dinner arrives, order the massive onion rings. Entree pricing runs the gamut from $9.95 to $24.95. If you are headed for Bagnell Dam, Boer also owns the Blue Heron (314–365–4646), which sits high atop a ridge overlooking the lake off Business 54 at State Road HH, less than ½ mile along the cliff. For cocktails outdoors by the lighted pool or continental dinner inside, the Heron is more upscale and elegant. In both places, Boer has one of the finest wine lists in the state. Both restaurants are closed from the middle of November until the third Friday in March.

If you have taken the route along the west side of the lake, you will begin to see the real Ozarks now. Missouri has surprisingly diverse wildlife, from the blind cave fish to the black bear, which still forages in the heavy woods. The pileated woodpecker (the size of a chicken, no kidding!) will certainly wake you up in the morning if he decides to peck on your shake shingles. The west side of the lake is still undiscovered except by Kansas City people, who have tried to keep it quiet. Here, great eating places abound and small shops hide off the beaten path.

Highway 5 cuts like a razor slash through the hills between Gravois Mills and Laurie. After Versailles and not quite to Gravois Mills you will pass **Lyman's** on Highway 5. You may notice bison grazing beside the place and a sign out front that reads: BUFFALO BILL ATE HIS FIRST BUFFALO BURGER SOMEWHERE; EAT YOUR FIRST BUFFALO BURGER HERE. If you wonder about the flavor that made the buffalo an endangered species, this is your chance. The restaurant and a campground sit on Gravois Creek, which feeds into the nearby Lake of the Ozarks. Call (314) 372–5626.

⊃**Spring Lake Lodge and Antiques** (314–372–2201), owned by James Marci and Gordon Stallings, is no flea market. Open March to October, the shop contains fine antiques, art objects, jewelry, and decorative accessories that are as nice as those at big-city shops but priced more reasonably. The shop is closed in the winter so that the two men can travel around the country finding and buying the elegant pieces they show there. People who know about the place try to be the first ones there in the spring when the shop opens. Large walnut sideboards, Victorian sofas, and unique lamps are part of the hundreds of items in the two floors of showroom.

As you continue along Highway 5 through the town of Gravois Mills, you will notice a large sign pointing to **Troutdale Ranch.** It is not the spot for experienced trout fishers, but it is the perfect spot to teach the children how to cast a line (guaranteed catch) *and* it is the perfect place to pick up some sweet, pink-fleshed trout for dinner. There has been a trout farm here since 1932. Current owner Dorothy Gates and her son Lorin haven't changed things much. Someone will simply go out the door and net you some of the freshest trout you will ever taste. They will clean and bone it for you and pack it in ice, too. The water here is fifty-six degrees, colder than most trout waters, so the trout grow more slowly and that means better. They are farm fed, making them safe and some of the best you will ever eat. Many of the best restaurants in the metropolitan areas serve trout from the ranch. Troutdale is open all year from 7:30 A.M. until 4:30 P.M. (from November until March 1, they are closed on Sunday). Call (314) 372–6100.

Just outside of Laurie on Highway 5 is **St. Patrick's Catholic Church.** Father Fred Barnett is the pastor here. This unique church sits on acres of outdoor gardens that feature waterfalls, fountains, and a shrine dedicated to mothers. You may add your mother's name to the list to be remembered in ongoing prayers. On summer Sundays, Mass is at 8:30 A.M. at the shrine, and casual dress is in the spirit of a Lake of the Ozarks vacation. The outdoor candlelight procession and Mass on Saturday nights at 8:30 P.M. at the shrine are beautiful and open to anyone. Times change in winter, so call Father Barnett (314–374–7855) for a current schedule.

Near the town of Greenview on Highway 5 stands a hand-hewn oak log building. Known as the Ɔ**Old Trail House** (314–873–5824), it overlooks the lake at the spot where one of the wagon trails going from Old Linn Creek to Arnholdt's Mill on the Big Niangua River ran across the ridge. Wagons drawn by oxen and horses forded the river at the mill. The spot is said to be an old Indian lookout point, and you can see for about 20 miles to the west from the deck, where dinner is served in good weather. A beautiful, antique oak mantel surrounds a log fire in winter. It is a favorite spot of locals.

If you are looking for a bed and breakfast instead of a resort on the Lake of the Ozarks, check with Kay Cameron at Ozark Mountain Country Bed and Breakfast Service at (800) 695–1546 or (417) 334–4720. Kay has listings for cottages on the water in Camdenton, Osage Beach, Sunrise Beach, and other small towns around the lake.

Either way you circle the lake, east or west, you will end up in Camdenton at the intersection of Highways 5 and 54, where you will see Piggy's Ice Cream Paradise, worth mentioning for the name alone. Continue west on Highway 54 and turn on Highway D to Ɔ**Ha Ha Tonka State Park.** High on a bluff overlooking an arm of the Lake of the Ozarks, poised over a cold, aqua blue spring that bubbles out from under a limestone bluff, are the ruins of a stone "castle" with a story to tell. There is a European feel to the ruins; it's as if you have stumbled on a Scottish stronghold here in the Missouri woods. The place was conceived in 1900 as a sixty-room retreat for prominent Kansas City business-man Robert Snyder. But tragedy struck; Snyder was killed in an automobile accident in 1906 and construction halted. Later, the castlelike mansion was completed by Snyder's son, but in 1942 a fire set by a spark from one of the many stone fireplaces gutted the buildings. All that was left were the ghostly stone walls thrust up against the sky. Ha Ha Tonka is now a state park, although the mansion is still a ghostly ruins half hidden in the trees.

Ha Ha Tonka

The park is a classic example of karst topography, with caves and sinkholes, springs, natural bridges, and underground streams. (This typical southern Missouri geology is responsible for the many caves in the state.) There are nine natural trails here; explore on your own or check in with the park office (314–751–2479) for a naturalist-guided tour; programs are available all year long.

While you're near Hickory County, make a quick run by the county seat. At Hermitage you'll find one of those typical, tiny limestone jails that make you shiver at the thought of incarceration. What makes this one different is that it was in use until 1985—brrr-r-r! Other than that, it's a cute town right out of the past century; the bandstand and the red-brick courthouse are charmers. Hermitage is tiny, however, and it is very poor; the town "square" has only three sides. Artist Margaret Boller has a shop here, where she teaches; she says one of the town's main attractions is the muzzle loaders' black-powder rendezvous in late summer, a great draw for history buffs.

About halfway between Warsaw and Clinton on Highway 7 is the town of Tightwad (population fifty-six) and the **Tightwad Tavern and B-B-Q** (816–477–3389). Owner Wayne Grigsby came to Tightwad in 1946 at the tender age of four. Now he chops wood and smokes meat. Hours are from 11:00 A.M. to 9:00 P.M. every day but Monday. The lounge has live music—country and good old-fashioned rock and roll—from 9:00 P.M. until 1:00 A.M., so you can get down and boogie, too. In winter months—January and February—he takes it easy and just opens Friday through Sunday.

The city of Clinton is every chamber of commerce's dream come true. It has one of the most active squares in the country, filled with over 150 shops and services, and there is lots of parking. You can't miss the wonderful old courthouse and outdoor pavilion in the center of the square. The town has changed little since 1836, when it began as an outpost in the heart of the Golden Valley.

Although never considered a battlefield, Clinton contained a Union military post, and it suffered from guerrilla raids and skirmishes. History buffs will find plenty of research material at the ↄ**Henry County Museum** at 203 West Franklin Street, just off the northwest corner of the square. The building itself was owned by Anheuser-Busch from 1886 until Prohibition. Huge blocks of ice (often cut from the nearby lake) were used to chill the kegs in the cooling room. The second room contains a skylight and double doors leading to the old loading dock and courtyard. Quick dashes in horse-drawn wagons were necessary to transport the beer while still cool to the depot where there was access to three railroads. The building houses the Courtenay Thomas room, commemorating the Clinton native who became an international operatic soprano.

You'll pass by Truman Dam and Reservoir as you head north; watch here, too, for eagles, or drop a line—you just might beat an eagle to a fish.

Find Commercial Street in Harrisonville and hit the antiques jackpot. There are too many antiques and flea markets to mention, but it looks like three cherries on the antiques slot machine for flea-market gamblers.

Cheese Country

Nevada (pronounced Na-VAY-da), south of Harrisonville on Highway 71, has a typical town square with the **Nevada Deli** (417–667–3850) on the east side. Owners Mike and Shirley Farran offer real deli delights—pastrami, corned beef, dark rye, and even New York seltzer—that are hard to find in the Midwest. Hours are 8:30 A.M. to 4:30 P.M. weekdays.

Here you can go west on Highway 54 to El Dorado Springs (Da-RAY-do, this being a very non-Spanish part of the country) as a shortcut to the Osceola area.

Large dairy barns and silos built around the turn of the century are still in use and dairy cattle—Holsteins and Guernseys—join beef cattle along the roadside. Surprise! Missouri is the third-largest cheese-producing state in the nation.

El Dorado Springs, just east of Nevada off Highway 54, is a pretty little town complete with a nostalgic bandstand in the tree-shaded park at the center of town. It looks like something straight out of *The Music Man.* There's a band here every Friday and Saturday night and Sunday afternoon; a local band has played in the park for over a hundred years. The old spa town was crowded with bathhouses and hotels, but the spa business ended long ago for most towns like this one. El Dorado Springs has done a great job of preserving itself anyway.

If you don't take the shortcut, you will continue down Inter-state 71 to **Lamar**; history fans will find ⊃**Harry S Truman's Birthplace** here. (No, there is no period after the S because the president didn't have a middle name—his folks just put an S in there.) It's a long way from this little house to the big white one on Pennsylvania Avenue in our nation's capital.

Bicyclists know a place called **Cooky's** at 825 Main in Golden City at the junction of Highways 126 and 37 south and east of Lamar. Out of season, it's a small-town cafe on the south side of the main drag. During bike-riding season, though, Cooky's is the place to dream about when you are 300 miles out on the trail. Bikecentennial, Inc., of Missoula, Montana, put Cooky's on the map—the Transamerica Trail map, that is, and riders have flocked here ever since for some serious carbohydrate loading. It's not uncommon to watch a rider from Australia chow down on three or four pieces of Jim and Carol Elred's terrific pies; you can be more moderate, if you like. A steak dinner costs only $7.50; the home-raised beef will keep you going down the trail whether you come by car or bike (417–537–4741).

Jerry Overton, president of the Missouri Prairie Foundation, puts in a good word for ⊃**Golden Prairie,** designated a National Natural Landmark by the Federal Department of the Interior. It's not reclaimed prairie or replanted prairie—this is a virgin rem-nant of the thousands of acres of grassland that once covered the Midwest, important not only for the historic plants it con-tains, but also for the varieties of wildlife that inhabit it. Here, you can still hear the sound of the prairie chickens. Listen for them exactly 3 miles west of Golden City on Highway 126 and exactly 2 miles south of Highway 26 on the first gravel road.

The ⊃**Bush Hotel** (antiques, bed and breakfast) in Jerico Springs north on Highway 97 is owned by Rodney and Renee Shipley (417–398–2343 or 398–2519 when the shop is closed). It was a run-down disaster when they found it, a relic of the min-eral spas popular about 1906 and the last survivor of the many hotels in town. Now it contains eight refurbished rooms with four bathrooms to share. A different country breakfast is served each morning—perhaps biscuits and gravy or waffles. Rooms are $40 for one night, $35 each additional night. The weekend nearest June 9 is busy every year because of the annual Jerico Springs picnic/reunion, but for the most part the hotel caters to folks headed for Stockton Lake because Highway B is the quickest route to the lake from Interstate 71. The shop is open Thursday through Saturday from 9:00 A.M. to 5:00 P.M.

⊃**Stockton Cheese Shop** owners Ezell and Alberta Goodwin in Stockton, at the northern tip of Stockton Lake at the Highway 32–39 junction, carry eighty-five varieties of cheese plus sorghum, honey, and coffee. They process much of the cheese themselves and are working on a manufacturing plant. Cheeses come from all over the world as well as from Missouri, and they'll ship cheese anywhere in the country by UPS or overnight mail, although they prefer not to in summer's heat. Call them at (800) 243–3738 or (417) 276–3618 in state. The shop has recently moved to 1411 South Street, eleven blocks south of the square.

A roadside park just outside Osceola on Highway 82 West will show you what attracted Indians and settlers to the area—the breathtaking view of the white bluffs where the Sac and Osage rivers meet. Highway 82 also has a Sac River access point and boat ramp if you are hauling a boat to the Truman reservoir.

Highway 13 bypasses the town square but is home to **Osceola Cheese** and **Ewe's in the Country** (417–646–8131). Mike and Marcia Bloom own both shops, which share the building. The Blooms buy the cheese in bulk and smoke and flavor it in the former cheese factory; they have been at this same location for over forty-five years. They now offer over sixty-nine varieties of cheese, mostly from Missouri, with each type cut for sampling. Try jalapeño (extra hot), instant pizza, or chocolate (yes!) cheese. Pick up a catalog; they ship cheese anywhere in the world— except from April to September, when it might arrive as hot cheese sauce. Hours are 7:00 A.M. to 8:00 P.M. weekdays at the cheese shop, 9:00 A.M. to 5:00 P.M. at the gift shop.

Take a right at the sign on Highway 13 and wander into Osceola. On the northeast corner of the town square is **Dempsey's Coach Stop.** There are many stories to be told here, if the walls could talk. With the help of artist M. E. Norton, they do. Harry Truman ate here, Jesse James slept here, and Dr. Ruth Seevers practiced here until she was ninety and had delivered more babies than anyone in the state. She died at 102, no doubt of exhaustion. The Butterfield Stage Line stopped here, and the Corps of Engineers built the Truman Dam nearby. Owners Ken and Donna Dempsey will explain each section of the montage if you are interested: the Seminole chief who never surrendered

(Chief Osceola), or the time the town was burned to the ground by Jim Lane, just after the Civil War—it's wall-to-wall history.

On the southwest corner of the square is the 109-year-old Commercial Hotel, now being renovated and opened as a craft shop. ⊃**Colby's Cafe,** at 107 Chestnut on the north side of the square (also in a renovated old building), is where Curtis and Kathy Colby serve from-scratch meals from 6:00 A.M. to 2:00 P.M. seven days a week. Kathy is from Kansas City and says that moving to Osceola took some adjusting. "But my four kids have seen bald eagles and deer they would only have seen in the zoo," she says. The pan-fried chicken on Wednesday and Sunday ($3.25) draws a crowd. Call (417) 646–2620.

Across the corner of the square is the Family Savings Center, an old-fashioned hardware store ("if we don't have it, you don't need it"), where you can meet "Gar" and Donnetta Garman. Gar writes for the *Osage Chiggar* and the *Otter,* local newspapers. His humor column under the pseudonym Red Necht (". . . it's not just a name, it's a condition—hard workin', honest common folk what lives on the Osage River 'tween Roscoe and Osceola . . . ," according to Red) is filled with local color and history.

Off the Beaten Path in Northwest Missouri

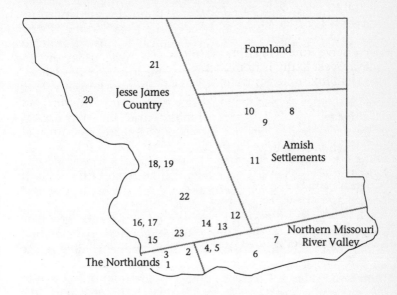

1. Coffee Gallery
2. Nichols Pottery Shop and Studio
3. Hodge Park
4. Corbin Mill Place
5. Martha Lafite Thompson Nature Sanctuary
6. Ray County Museum
7. museum of hammers
8. Jamesport
9. McDonald's Tea Room
10. Adam-Ondi-Ahman Shrine
11. J. C. Penney Memorial Library and Museum
12. Excelsior Springs
13. Watkins Woolen Mill State Historic Site
14. Jesse James Farm Historic Site
15. English Landing
16. McCormick Distilling Company
17. The Vineyards
18. Albrecht Art Museum
19. St. Joseph Hospital Psychiatric Museum
20. Squaw Creek National Wildlife Refuge
21. Conception Abbey
22. Candyman's Mule Barn
23. Smithville Lake

Northwest Missouri

It gets cold in northwest Missouri—make no mistake—especially near the northernmost border, where the plains are chilled by every stiff wind howling down from the frigid north. Alberta Clipper, Siberian Express, whatever you call it, Missouri catches hell in the winter, bringing to mind that old joke: "There's nothing between here and the North Pole but two bobwire fences, and one o' *them's* down." In 1989 all records were broken—along with that fence—when the nighttime temperature bottomed out at minus twenty-three degrees (wind chill made that sixty degrees below zero). It also gets hot in Missouri; August days can soar over the hundred-degree mark.

But at its temperate best, Jesse James Country is a great place to visit that's filled with great hideouts. (James knew them all. It seems that, like George Washington, Jesse James slept almost everywhere—in northwest Missouri anyway.)

Not that that's all there is to this section of the state; we'd hate to say we're living in the past on the rather unsavory reputation of our own "Robbing" Hood. There is a national wildlife refuge on the central flyway that is absolutely essential to migrating waterfowl. There is Excelsior Springs, where folks once came to take the waters and where Harry S Truman heard he had lost the presidential election to Thomas Dewey—at least according to the *Chicago Tribune*.

You'll find the J. C. Penney Museum. You'll find Conception Abbey, where the monks print a line of greeting cards to rival the big boys who "care enough to print the very best." The "weather monk" also lives here. And the deep winter cold is just fine for skiing Snow Creek.

You can buy a Stetson hat at the factory in St. Joseph, or visit the museum that celebrates the jumping-off point for the Pony Express. Find a reconstruction of a Native American ceremonial site at Smithville Lake, or visit any number of places that commemorate the colorful career of everyone's favorite outlaw. (Yep, it's Jesse again; here we have his birthplace, his grave, various robbery sites, and the place where he was gunned down by "that dirty little coward that shot Mr. Howard . . . . ")

The Northlands

North Kansas City is just across the Missouri River from the town with a similar name. This is a separate city, with a healthy industrial tax base and a coordinated downtown shopping area complete with plazas, fountains, and wide streets. "Northtown" has its own mayor, its own police department, and its own quirky charm. There are cafes and delis and bakeries; North Kansas Citians know how to eat.

Imagine a frigid winter's morning when you curse the mere necessity of leaving your bed; now imagine salvation. No, it's not Saturday; it's **Gunther's Bakery** at 308 Armour Road (816–842– 9049), open Monday through Friday from 5:00 A.M. to 1:00 P.M. A cup of Gunther's steaming coffee and any one of a dozen unbelievable pastries will make all seem right with the world; the apple turnovers are heaven. (Of course, this is also the place to stop on a hot summer morning, or a spring afternoon, or . . .) Steven McPhetters is the baker; do you suppose he was born with that talent?

What's that delightful aroma? No, it's not the Folger's plant just south across the river, though it could be when the wind is right. You're on the right scent, though—it's the **⊃Coffee Gallery** at 305 Armour Road (816–842–2414), and what you detect is the fragrance of hundreds of flavored coffees and teas from all over the world. Charming gift baskets are available to let you share the wealth. Sherry Thompson is the owner; ask her to recommend her favorite blends.

Pastimes Eats and Drinks cooks up just plain good food at 312 Armour Road (816–842–3869). Owner Michael Donovan offers a great batch of chili (chili fans will appreciate this doctor-it-up-as-you-like-it dish), old-fashioned hot beef sandwiches drowned in savory gravy, or nostalgic favorites from the antique soda fountain.

Before you leave Northtown you might want to browse around the **Olde Bellas Hess Antique Mall** at 715 Armour Road (816–474–4790) in one of the oldest buildings north of the river. Now the old catalog store is filled with thousands of rare antiques and hard-to-find collectibles. Hours are Monday through Saturday from 10:00 A.M. till 6:00 P.M. and Sunday from noon till 5:00 P.M., and the coffee in the coffee shop is free.

Tiny Avondale is slightly off of Highway 210 as you leave North Kansas City. Here you'll discover ↄ**Nichols Pottery Shop and Studio** at 2615 Bell (816–452–0880). Deanna Nichols handcrafts stoneware that is both beautiful and functional. "You can hang it on a wall, or take it down and serve from it," she says. The studio is filled with examples of her work—not only mugs and platters, but also intricate, earthy fountains some 32 inches high. She does custom work, lamps, and dinnerware. Browse through the shop Tuesday through Saturday from 10:00 A.M. to 5:00 P.M.

As long as you are here, check out **Avondale Furniture and Antiques** at 2600 North Highway 10. Hours are catch-as-catch-can; call (816) 452–2690 for an appointment if you prefer. Owner Lillian Waskovsky has an auction service and warehouse and likes to move pieces quickly. This place may not be glitzy, but the prices are very right.

Take the Highway 435 exit north off Interstate 35 and keep an eye out for Highway 152. A right turn will take you to ↄ**Hodge Park,** a fine place to get away from the "two Ps"—progress and people.

Those big, hairy critters you spot as you enter the park are American bison; the Kansas City Zoo maintains a small herd here, where once there were thousands. Elk and deer share the enclosure; you may be able to get "up close and personal" with some of the Midwest's largest indigenous animals (well, a chain-link fence apart, anyway).

If human history is more your thing, park your car in the lot and keep walking. Shoal Creek, Missouri (816–444–4363), is a restored frontier town at Hodge Park, full of historic buildings moved here by the Kansas City Parks and Recreation Department. The tiny, two-story jail built of monolithic limestone blocks (how did they lift those things?) came from nearby Missouri City. What a place for a lockup! Local ne'er-do-wells slept off Saturday night festivities here some one hundred years ago. Other buildings include square-hewn log cabins, a one-room schoolhouse, a barn, a replica of an old mill complete with mill wheel and race, and some pretty fine houses for the gentry. Stop by during one of their living history weekends for a re-creation of frontier life; you'll feel as if you've stepped back a century. Fine nature trails lead into the woods from Shoal Creek.

If you are interested in archaeology and the peoples that inhabited this land before Europeans moved in, get yourself to **Line**

Creek Park at 5940 Northwest Waukomis. This is a Hopewell Culture site, where Native Americans lived and worked from approximately 50 B.C. to A.D. 200. The museum houses artifacts found on the spot and in the surrounding areas.

The Kansas City Parks and Recreation Department operates the site, and schoolchildren from grade four up come for mock "digs" (artifacts are salted back into the ground so that the kids have the excitement of discovery). Hours may vary; call (816) 444-4363, or take your chances—the museum is usually open Saturdays and Sundays from 11:00 A.M. to 4:00 P.M. There's no charge for the museum, but for reservations for group programs, call the above number; there is a small fee for groups.

Northern Missouri River Valley

Head east back on Highway 152 and you'll come to historic Liberty. The downtown square has been restored to Civil War–era glory, with authentic paint colors and fancy trim—most of it original.

On the south side of the square is the **Hardware Cafe** (816–792–3500), the latest incarnation of the old Boggess Hardware Store. Soups and salads are hearty and delicious, and entrees are never boring; if you like tea-room-style food and plenty of it, this is the place. Dessert lovers skip the meal and go right for the goodie tray. Try the "Robert Redford"—we won't tell you what's in it, but once you sink your teeth into this confection you'll never miss the real thing. Prices are reasonable; two can lunch for just over $10. There is a charming shop in the same building with the cafe for browsing (and buying); if there's a wait for your table, they will page you during your shopping.

The restored ⊃**Corbin Mill Place** (816–781–3100) is now a compendium of eight specialty shops housed in an old brick mill, among them Sandy's Antiques and a terrific selection of fabrics and supplies (as well as classes) at the Liberty Quilt Shoppe. Under the same roof is The Place to Eat; they make a fabulous Reuben sandwich, and prices are moderate.

Sandy and Tom Williams opened the mill in 1986 as an outgrowth of their original antiques store a few blocks away, and now they offer a great place to spend an afternoon—it just keeps growing. The mill, with its 24-inch-thick limestone foundation and 18-inch brick walls, is built on an original land grant from President James Monroe for relief from the 1811 New Madrid earthquake (that event had far-reaching consequences!). Corbin Mill Place is open at 131 South Water from 10:00 A.M. to 5:00 P.M. Monday through Saturday.

There are three museums in downtown Liberty, either on the square or within easy walking distance, among them the Jesse James Bank Museum Historic Site and the Mormon Jail Museum. The town is chock-full of antiques and craft shops, so plan on browsing. You can pick up a map at Corbin Mill.

A couple of blocks east of the square is William Jewell College, one of the top ten small colleges in the country according to *U.S. News and World Report*. It's a lovely old campus of warm brick; the original buildings are still in daily use. Georgian architecture surrounds the quadrangle where the ornate brick water tower, erected with the first building in 1849, still stands. From 1861 to 1868 the Civil War closed the school, and Jewell Hall was used by Union troops as a hospital and stable. The cemetery on campus reflects this history, and its tombstones are a mirror of the times: Epidemics, baby deaths, wars, and consecutive wives lost to childbirth are all represented. Interestingly, the clergyman father of Frank and Jesse James made a generous financial pledge toward the founding of the college; after his death, his outlaw sons made good that pledge.

The ↺**Martha Lafite Thompson Nature Sanctuary** (816–781–8598) offers a wonderful place to watch the wildlife, take a naturalist-guided walk, or enjoy special programs—from making your own bird feeder to learning about the constellations on a night hike. Over 600 species of plants and many fish, reptiles, amphibians, and mammals make their homes here, and over 160 species of birds have been sighted. Worn out? Take in the lovely new sanctuary building with its displays of indigenous plants, or watch snapping turtles and catfish in the creek-habitat aquarium. Relax on the spacious deck in redwood Adirondack chairs, or buy a book or bird call to take home. Watch for the sanctuary sign at 407 North La Frenz Road.

Take Highway 210 through the tiny towns of Missouri City, Orrick, Fleming, and Camden, which are dotted along the Missouri River. The views are spectacular, especially from the observation stop just this side of Missouri City. At your back is

Nebo Hill, an important site for prehistoric Indians who found this a perfect place for ceremonies and camps; the site was in use for hundreds of years. After a good spring rain you're liable to see artifact hunters out in the fields nearby.

As you pass through tiny Missouri City, watch for the AAA-rated stone elementary school that has reaped national attention in *Reader's Digest* and *Newsweek;* it is one school that really works.

Highway 210 will take you to Richmond. Here the ⊃**Ray County Museum** occupies a beautiful old brick home on West Royle Street (816–776–2305). The Y-shaped building is unusual in itself, and the contents will tell you much about this area, from pre–Civil War days to the present. A special natural history section highlights indigenous wildlife.

To find the museum, go past the four-way stop at the edge of town on Highway 210 to Royle Street, and west to the large brick building atop the hill on the left. The library is open Wednesday through Sunday from noon until 4:00 P.M., but call for the new museum hours, which changed after its recent remodeling. If you are here the first weekend in October, you'll find mountain men, trappers, and traders as well as old-time arts and crafts at the Old Trails Festival on the grounds of the museum.

Richmond is also home to several unusual shops scattered around the area. **Garner Settle's Old House** (816–776–2378) is filled with eighteenth-century antiques at 607 North Thornton (look for the big red mailbox); it is open by chance or by appointment. Five miles north on Highway 13 is **The Farmer's Daughter Antiques** owned by Bob and Rilla Simmons (816–776–2936). Here you will find country furniture and all kinds of Americana, Monday through Friday from 11:00 A.M. to 4:00 P.M. and weekends by chance. About ½ mile beyond is **Country Cabin Crafts** (816–776–5636), where owner Janet Duncan keeps shop Wednesday to Friday from 11:00 A.M. to 4:00 P.M. (or Saturday through Tuesday by chance). To find Janet, turn right on the gravel road at Dockery and go 1 mile east. Follow the signs.

Just up Highway 10 between Richmond and Carrollton is a ⊃**museum of hammers** in Norborne. Yes, you heard right—hammers. Glen Albrecht has a shed full of them. This semi-retired farmer with a terrific sense of humor has collected hammers of all shapes, sizes, and applications and displays them neatly hung and labeled. It's an amazing array, as visitors from all over—including Europe and Japan—will attest. Glen insists it's not really a museum, just a collection. It's a *big* one. Admission is free, but hours are catch-as-catch-can at 405 Elmwood. Call Glen at (816) 594–3455 to make sure he's not out on the "north forty."

Amish Settlements

Chillicothe is a very special small town; don't pass it by. Barb Spencer has turned her problem—an allergy to almost everything—into an asset. She works in her home and has opened **The Enchanted Attic,** a delightful little shop with Victorian decor. Barb makes exquisite cloth dolls from things old and new; each is unique and meticulously crafted. She specializes in holiday dolls and dressed animals. Doll collectors note: These are museum quality. She also makes counted cross-stitch and other fine crafts. Call (816) 646–0009 for directions.

Remember that gorgeous blond of 1930s movies fame, Jean Harlow? The folks in Chillicothe do, every time they dine at **Harlow's** (816–646–6812). The lady's photos adorn every wall, reminding us what glamour was all about. It's tablecloth dining at 609 Jackson, but it's casual. Try the blue-ribbon–winning butter-fried turkey breast. Entrees range from $5.95 to $13.95.

North on Highway 65 is the town of Trenton. Don't mistake Trenton Cemetery Prairie for a neglected eyesore, with its rough grasses obscuring some of the old tombstones. Established in 1830, its protected status as a cemetery happily resulted in one of the few precious parcels of native prairie remaining in the state. Today it is maintained by the Missouri Conservation Department. Preservation is especially crucial; prairie north of the Missouri River is scarce. These patchwork remnants produce the seeds adapted to the northern Missouri climate that are essential to reestablishing prairie ecosystems.

This is an area of oddities; what you see may not be what you get. Riverside Country Club (816–359–6004), Trenton's golf course, has tree stumps carved into life-size animals around the fairways. (If you hit a birdie or an eagle around here, it may be a wooden one.) Former greens keeper Don McNabb was an artist with a chainsaw and has salted the nine-hole course with bears and other critters. The country club is open for golf to anyone from out of the county for the cost of a green fee (and cart rental, if you wish), but nongolfers are welcome to check out the carvings.

What's it like to live like a governor? You can find out for yourself. Hosts Robert and Carolyn Brown offer lodging in former Governor Arthur Hyde's mansion at 418 East Seventh Street (816–359–5631). The 1950s **Hyde Mansion Bed and Breakfast** was completely renovated by the Browns. The large dining room contains several small tables for more intimate breakfasts. Carolyn takes individual orders for country breakfasts, unless there is a full house. Then a buffet breakfast is served from the commercial-size kitchen. There are five bedrooms; the living room and its baby grand piano are all yours. Rooms, all with private baths, are $55 to $85. Hyde's is near enough to Jamesport to fill up on festival weekends, so make your reservations early.

Crowder State Park, just northwest of Trenton off Highway 146, is named after Major General Enoch H. Crowder, the Missouri native who founded the Selective Service System—better known as the draft. Don't dodge this one—it's a nice place for a picnic.

A short detour up Highway 65 to Princeton will take you to the birthplace of Martha Jane Canary, better known as Calamity Jane. Every fall (the third weekend in September) a four-day festival commemorates this feisty woman who needed no liberation. One feature of the festival used to be a public "hanging," but one year it nearly went too far. Something went wrong, and no one realized that the hangee wasn't just one heck of a good actor; he was almost a dead actor. That particular highlight has been dropped from the festival, but you can still watch a melodrama, a shoot-out, a parade, and an antique car show.

⊃**Jamesport** is a different world. It is the largest Mennonite settlement in Missouri and home to the most orthodox "horse and buggy" Mennonites. Here the Amish wear black, fasten clothes with pins, and allow no electricity in their homes. Don't ask the Amish to pose for pictures, though; it's against their beliefs.

The **Doll House** is a great B&B if you happen to love toys. The owner does, and she furnishes the place with all the goodies you remember from your childhood. She owns a doll shop in Kansas; reach her at (913) 432–2939, or call (816) 684–6333 for reservations. The Doll House was once the doctor's home in Jamesport; it has a history that almost everyone in town shares. It was an elegant home compared to the simple farmhouses nearby, and it was finished inside with fine oak woodwork.

There are over fifty shops in Jamesport, but only one of the Amish businesses, **Anna's Bake Shop,** is actually inside the city limits; even so, the bakery's address is Route 1. Pick up a map to the Amish shops and attractions at any of the town's businesses. The **Rolling Hills Store** offers sturdy dry goods at excellent prices (talk about natural fiber fabrics!), plus boots and shoes. Sherwood Quilts and Crafts has a bed piled high with handmade quilts; dig through till you find the one you can't live without. Gardeners, don't miss **Mast Greenhouse,** where you can stock your herb garden with aromatic plants that are as healthy as they come. **H & M Country Store** is a bulk-foods store with spices, herbs, and any kind of noodle you desire; the emphasis is on health and freshness. You may have noticed that no phone numbers are included; the Amish don't have 'em, making that map essential.

Don't overlook the regular businesses in town, especially if you're hungry. The Mennonite-owned **Gingerich Dutch Pantry Restaurant and Bakery** (816–684–6212) can fix you a big, Amish-style meal, then take you on a tour around the area; it is open from Monday to Saturday 6:00 A.M. to 9:00 P.M. Early birds may want to try the **Country Cupboard,** Tuesday to Sunday 6:00 A.M. to 9:00 P.M.

Gallatin has always been another favorite day trip for folks from the Kansas City area, mainly because of ⊃McDonald's Tea Room (816–663–2021), known to generations of Missourians. There is just something about this place that draws a crowd—people drive miles to eat here. It could be the great home cooking, or the quiet ambience. Or it *could* be the strawberry shortcake done in layers of pastry and buried in whipped cream. Look for McDonald's big sign on Grand Street—this one isn't golden arches. The tea room is open 11:00 A.M. to 8:00 P.M. Monday through Saturday and 11:00 A.M. to 4:00 P.M. Sunday.

The Mormons settled in western Daviess County in the 1830s. Just north and west of Gallatin (take Highway 13 north and turn west on Highway P) is the historic ⊃**Adam-Ondi-Ahman Shrine,** believed by Mormons to be the place where Christ will return. Northwest Missouri is important historically to the Mormon people; there were once thousands of them here. The majority were forced out during the Mormon Wars, where the state militia was ordered to drive them out of Missouri. The town of Far West, now no more than a historical marker, was comprised of 5,000 souls, all exterminated or driven from their homes. Many died during a forced march in this land of religious freedom. The marker is off Highway 13, west on Highway HH and north on Highway D, near Shoal Creek (just northwest of Kingston).

Goat Mountain Antiques and Crafts (816–663–2718) is ½ mile east of Gallatin on Highway 6; it's a must-stop if you like a good story and reasonable antiques, primitives, baskets, and hand-woven rugs. A hermit once lived on Goat Mountain between two main roads, with a railroad track nearby; in order to train his goats to stay out of danger, he popped them with a slingshot. The area still bears the name, in his honor—or his goats'. Now Bill and RoDonna Collier occupy the hill, and Ina Wright manages the shop from 10:00 A.M. to 5:30 P.M. everyday except Thursday and Sunday.

Ever wonder where retail giant J. C. Penney got his start? No, not New York, or even Chicago. It was right here in Hamilton in 1895 that he got his first job at Hale's Department Store. By the time he returned to Hamilton to buy his old employer's place of business in 1924, it was number 500 in his chain of stores. The motto of the J. C. Penney Company was "Honor, confidence, service and cooperation"—no wonder he did so well.

The ⊃**J. C. Penney Memorial Library and Museum** (816–583–9997), uptown on Davis Street, is open Tuesday through Saturday from 10:00 A.M. to 5:00 P.M. You'll love the displays of early merchandise—makes you wonder who wore the stuff. The Penney farm cottage has also been restored by the city of Hamilton.

Even cattlemen like this area's history. J. C. Penney once raised great herds of Angus, and at the Penney farm there is a monument—a big monument—to Penney's prize bull.

Jesse James Country

Take the Business 69 exit to ⊃**Excelsior Springs.** Once a magnet for people who wished to "take the waters," this old spa has enough moxie to try for a comeback. The health-spa ship was scuttled in the 1950s when an article in the *Saturday Evening Post* declared mineral waters an ineffective form of treatment; the demise was clinched when Missouri passed a bill prohibiting

Jesse James
Farm

Mineral
Water
Well,
Excelsior
Springs

Tryst
Falls

Octagonal Schoolhouse,
Watkins Mill

Elms Hotel,
Excelsior
Springs

Attractions in and around Excelsior Springs

advertising by doctors, so now we enjoy the waters—and the baths and massages—for the lovely, hedonistic fun of it.

Visit the Hall of Waters at 201 East Broadway, the world's longest mineral-water bar, and sample some of the waters that attracted thousands near the turn of the century. There are more naturally occurring types of mineral waters here than anyplace else on earth except the German city of Baden-Baden, which ties Excelsior Springs.

For a truly sybaritic experience, check the schedule for baths and massage, also at the Hall of Waters (816–637–0752); Horace Holmes operates the newly restored spa. The lovely Art Deco–style building, built in 1937 as "the finest and most complete health resort structure in the U.S.," is a fine example of a WPA project begun during the Great Depression. Moreover, how many towns have city offices that are shared with mineral baths and massage rooms—not to mention a 25-meter indoor pool (which may be reopened by the time you read this)?

What do Harry S Truman, Al Capone, and Franklin D. Roosevelt have in common? They all stayed at the **Elms Hotel** (816–637–2141) at Elms Boulevard and Regent Street. You can too; the hotel was rescued from bankruptcy in 1979 and restored to provide a spa experience in English Tudor surroundings. Visit the environmental rooms with their saunas, hot tubs, and gentle, rainlike showers; take a steam bath and massage; stuff yourself at a sumptuous Sunday brunch in the ballroom; take a surrey ride around town; or just enjoy the beautiful grounds—artists often choose this area to hone their skills.

There are nice little antiques shops along Thompson Avenue, the main street leading into downtown Excelsior Springs, and down a few blocks on Broadway. At 413 Thompson, Louise and Mack Dison run the **L & M Shoppe,** the kind of old-fashioned operation where it's easy to strike a wonderful bargain (not an easy trick in antiques malls where the booth owner may be three counties away). It's open 10:00 A.M. till 5:00 P.M. Monday through Saturday.

If hunger strikes while you're antiquing, back up a little to **Back in Time,** Richard and Clara Bloss's new offering at 439 Thompson. Here, you'll find antiques—forty booths in all—plus good, good food. The breads and desserts are all homemade, the soups will make you think of Mom's, and the dijon chicken salad is to die for. Try the bread pudding, or the peach crisp. Or order a day ahead and take home a loaf of wonderful bread—flavor of your choice—fresh and still warm from the oven.

Back in Time (816–637–4565) is open from 8:00 A.M. to 5:00 P.M. Monday, Wednesday, and Friday; 8:00 A.M. till 2:00 P.M. Tuesday and Saturday; and 8:00 A.M. till 8:00 P.M. on Thursday. In case you can't think of anything for Thursday dinner, Clara can!

North of the stop sign and down a block at 109 West Broadway, check Laura Kingery's and Bob Whitacre's **Barter House** (816–637–3532) for goodies from rare antique books to used kitchen utensils. Tuffy the dog will greet you joyously—she loves attention. There are booths and booths here; where does it all *come* from? Browse Monday through Saturday from 10:00 A.M. till 5:00 P.M.

The Old Bank Museum, 101 East Broadway (816–637–3712), preserves spa-town history. (Check out the dentist's office and thank your lucky stars this is the 1990s.) Look up to find a pair of murals; they're wonderful copies of Jean-François Millet's *The Gleaners* and *The Angelus,* painted by an itinerant artist with more talent than fame. You can buy postcards, homemade lye soap, or a museum membership (for $1.00); you may find the Women's Auxiliary of the museum quilting or weaving rag rugs when you visit on a Wednesday. The chamber of commerce is here; Sally Dixon will fill you in on local happenings.

For an elegant retreat without the bustle of a large hotel, stay at **Crescent Lake Manor Bed and Breakfast,** 1261 Louis Avenue (816–637–2958), a moat-encircled, colonial-style estate built at the turn of the century. There are twenty-one gardenlike acres to stroll in; more active types may swim in the large pool or play a fast game of tennis on the estate's courts. Rates are $55 to $65, and there are senior and corporate rates. A full breakfast is included, and pickup from Kansas City International Airport or the Amtrak station in downtown Kansas City is available.

For a straight shot back to Kansas City, you can take Highway 69 west; but do plan to stop along the way at the **Old Crockery Restaurant and Antiques** (816–635–9058) near Mosby, a mile or 3 outside of Excelsior Springs. This place sits beside glassy lakes where you can fish, walk, camp, or just sit and enjoy the geese and cormorants and herons—or whatever other opportunistic birds have found the pay fishing lakes; the birds fish free. The restaurant used to be billed as Steak and Bait, with a nod to the pay lakes; somehow this is more appetizing, though you can still get bait nearby. The food is good, country-style, and plentiful; you can buy Amish bulk goods here, as well. When you're done, browse among the antiques for a fun experience all in one place.

If you have a bit longer, turn west off Highway 69 onto Highway 92 to Watkins Mill State Park near Lawson. Follow the signs to the Ꜿ**Watkins Woolen Mill State Historic Site** and get ready to walk back in time. The decades fall away like leaves as you wander down the footpath from the parking area. You pass deep Missouri woods, then a tiny stone-walled cemetery where the gravestones are encrusted with lichen. Farther along the path a brick giant rises to your right, and a graceful mansion crowns the hill to your left. A young belle could make quite an entrance down the lovely, curved walnut staircase in the entryway—and probably did, more than once.

Waltus Watkins built his empire here around 1850, in the years before the Civil War. Quite an empire it was: The three-story brick mill employed dozens, providing woolen fabrics to the area. The milling machinery, from washing vats to looms, is still intact, providing pristine examples of early industrial ingenuity. The house and its outbuildings reflect a gracious life—the reward for hard work and hard-headed business sense.

Before it became a state park, the mill seemed destined for destruction. The family was selling it after more than a century of occupancy, and the place was on the auction block. Representatives from the Smithsonian were on hand to bid on rare equipment—but the day was saved, along with the integrity of the mill complex, when private individuals bought the site lock, stock, and barrel (and there were a few of those about). Eventually they were able to pass the mill complex along to the state of Missouri, and now you can tour the mill and the elegant home on the hill, participate in living history weekends (try not to miss the Victorian Christmas), or watch an ongoing archaeological dig intended to discover still more about day-to-day life one hundred years ago and more. Tours are given Monday through Saturday from 10:00 A.M. till 4:00 P.M. and Sunday from 11:00 A.M. till 4:00 P.M. Winter hours are 11:00 A.M. till 4:00 P.M. Admission is $1.25 for adults, and 75 cents for children under twelve. Special events, like Lost Arts festivals and Christmas programs, are usually free. A new interpretive center opened in 1992 and acts as museum and buffer between now and the nineteenth century.

A brick church and an octagonal schoolhouse are nearby, all restored to their original condition. The Watkins children and those of mill workers and local farmers attended to their readin', 'ritin', and 'rithmetic here. See the schoolhouse when it's open, if you can; call (816) 296–3357. The ventilation system of windows high in the octagonal clerestory turret is ingenious. Sunlight reflects softly around the white-painted walls inside; not much artificial light would have been necessary, with the tall windows on every side.

Back on Highway 92 (a narrow, winding highway that's far from an interstate in character if not in miles) watch for the TRYST FALLS PARK sign. This is an important geologic feature of the region, being an outcropping of the Bethany Falls limestone common to much of the Midwest (although in drought years you might call it "Tryst No Falls" instead).

Once the site of an old mill, the falls is still a lovely place to picnic. Tables are snugged into a huge, natural amphitheater where the limestone has eroded over the centuries; you're protected from the wind from three directions here. The Clay County Parks Department also provides softball fields and tennis courts. The park closes at twilight; in the winter that can be as early at 4:30 P.M.

History buffs should look for the ⊃**Jesse James Farm Historic Site** (816–635–6065) just off Highway 92 on Jesse James Drive, between Excelsior Springs and Kearney (watch for signs). The white house with its gingerbread trim and cedar roof sits just over a rise, a little way back from the road; the new asphalt drive and path make the place handicapped accessible. The original part of the house is a log cabin, which was recently rescued from a precarious slide into decay. The cabin contains, among other things, the remains of Jesse's original coffin, which was exhumed when the body was moved to nearby Kearney; the family originally buried him in the yard to keep the body from being disturbed by those bent on revenge or souvenirs. The coffin is odd by today's standards; there was a glass window at face level—presumably for viewing the body, not for providing a window on eternity for the deceased!

The newer section of the house was a Sears Roebuck mail order. Mrs. James decided that the old place was getting too run down—not to mention crowded—and she sent for the two-room addition, assembled on the spot. It still sports the original wallpaper.

This is the famous outlaw's birthplace, the place where his

father was hanged and his mother's arm was lost to a Pinkerton's bomb. Enjoy the new on-site museum, which includes a gift shop full of James memorabilia, books, and local crafts, or stick around in August and September for the play, *The Life and Times of Jesse James.* Oh, yes—brother Frank was there, too.

Admission for the museum and home is $2.50 for adults, $2.25 for seniors, and $1.00 for children six to twelve. Summer hours are from 9:00 A.M. to 4:00 P.M. seven days a week; winter's cold, short days call for slightly reduced hours on weekends: from noon to 4:00 P.M.

On a less grim note, visit the Claybrook Mansion across the road from the James Farm. This delightful pre–Civil War home owned by Jesse's daughter and her husband was the last word in modern convenience and elegance. Fairs and historic re-creations bring Claybrook alive several times a year. Purchase tickets at the James Farm; the price is included in James Farm tour admission, but it is open only during warm weather; the place is like a barn to heat.

And if you've ever wanted to lay a flower on the outlaw's grave, it's located in Mt. Olivet Cemetery on Highway 92, ½ mile east of Interstate 35 in Kearney (pronounced CAR-ney). Look for it near the cedar trees at the west end of the cemetery, which is open during daylight hours year round.

Legend has it that Jesse, Frank, and/or Cole Younger visited darn near every fallen-down log cabin in this part of Missouri— not to mention the surrounding states. The James gang would have had to be in three places at once, the way their exploits were reported, but no matter. That's the fun thing about legends; they're much more elastic than the truth.

Fast-growing Kearney still hangs on to its small-town charm. At **Clem's Cafe,** 119 East Washington (816–635–4044), Charlie Davis (not Clem—you'll have to ask Charlie for that story) serves great homemade pies; in fact, everything is homemade.

Country Peddler Antiques at 108 West Washington (816–635–6030) is full of wonderful stuff; owner Mary Griffith has added a new room to the west and plans to fill a second story as well. Hours Monday through Saturday are 10:00 A.M. to 5:00 P.M. The shop was closed for a while, so if you missed the Peddler, try, try again.

Just one block north of the junction of Highways 33 and 92, you'll find a delightful place; The **Hospitality House** lives up to its name in a big two-story home. At lunch salads, sandwiches, and specials won't disappoint you, and if you're lucky, the hearty baked potato soup will be on the menu. Desserts are marvelous. For something different, owners Bob and Fern Buhlig invite you to Sunday dinner. There's no menu; you just pick from Grandma's Old-Fashioned Pan-Fried Chicken Dinner or Grandpa's Favorite Roast Beef Dinner. There's plenty of it, and it's so good you'll imagine yourself back on the farm. Open from 11:00 A.M. to 2:00 P.M. for lunch and 5:00 P.M. to 8:00 P.M. for dinner Tuesdays through Saturdays, and from 11:00 A.M. to 2:30 P.M. for that Sunday dinner.

A few doors down is **Jefferson Street Antiques,** open from 10:00 A.M. to 5:00 P.M. Thursday through Saturday; "other days, maybe," says owner Marilyn Daugherty. The Victorian home is filled to overflowing with goodies, as are the shed and barn and garage.

At 200 South Prospect, you will see an 1898 Victorian house with a huge bear in the yard (holding a sign that says OPEN if you are lucky). Here Reiko Schroff and Tammy Long create hand-crafted wooden expressions at **Bear in the Wood** (816–635–5725). Folk art, quilt stands and needlework frames, reproduction stools and benches, kitchen aids, children's items, barbed wire art (!), and a wide variety of finished and unfinished wooden things fill the shop.

Mt. Gilead Church and Academy Historic Site is a picturesque, white country church and school with an adjoining historic graveyard. Take Highway 92 about 3 miles west of Interstate 35 and turn right on the third road past the interstate. It's a wonderful place for a box lunch and a bit of quiet; children from local schools sometimes spend a day here discovering what learning the "three Rs" in the last century was like; if you're lucky, you'll stop by when class is in session and the kids are dressed like Tom Sawyers and Becky Thatchers. From here, Interstate 35 will take you back to Kansas City.

Watch along Highway 9 beside the Missouri River for huge limestone bluffs with streaks of shale and chert and narrow ribbons of coal; you're seeing prehistory. Highway 9 will lead you to the charming little college town of Parkville. This is a bustling crafts and antiques center, with long-time shops interwoven with new establishments. ⊃**English Landing,** across the tracks from the old town, houses the Parkville Fine Arts Gallery (816–741–7270), a great place to look for original paintings, pottery, or jewelry; the gallery features an "artist of the month," allowing for plenty of variety. In business for over twenty years, it's run by an association of artists. Sort of debunks the "flighty artist" stereotype, doesn't it? Open Tuesday through Saturday 10:30 A.M. to 5:00 P.M. and Sunday 1:00 P.M. to 5:00 P.M.

Also included in this complex is **The Old Mill Emporium,** an arts and crafts center that rents out booth space to a wide spectrum of crafters. Call (816) 741–5990 for information.

Just past the shopping complex is quiet English Landing Park on the banks of the Missouri. Look for the historic ninety-one-year-old Waddell "A" truss bridge, one of only two of this type left in the country. It was recently salvaged and moved to its present location. Now it's the focal point of the park, providing a walkway across a small feeder creek leading to the big river.

Cecil Doubenmier (816–587–9286) is a prize-winning Parkville potter who sells mostly at craft fairs—there's not room at his place for visitors. But if you don't want to follow him around the Midwest, look for his work at the **Peddler's Wagon,** a downtown quilt shop.

Cottonwoods and Willows at 112½ Main Street not only offers gifts and accessories, but owners Mary Ann Harvey and Donna Cholak have trimmed the upstairs of the 140-year-old Cottonwoods and Willows building with honeysuckle garlands and converted it into the Garden Tea Room. Donna makes interesting soups (the curried carrot is a favorite), sandwiches, and quiches. Lunch is served from 11:30 A.M. to 3:00 P.M., desserts and coffee from 3:00 P.M. to 5:00 P.M. Tuesday through Sunday. The tea room is available for dinner and private parties by reservation; call (816) 587–9093.

The newest excitment in Parkville (so new, in fact, that it might not even be there yet!) is the brand new **Casino Showboat.** Missouri's recently-passed riverboat gambling legislation now allows casinos to ply the Missouri and Mississippi rivers with roulette wheels, video poker, craps tables, slot machines, and blackjack. K. C. Stanley is owner of the new packet boat, a replica of the original Showboat. She says there will be food and drink on board and hopes to have it cruising down the river sometime in 1993. It will leave from the pier at 200 South Main and run all day and most of the night every day of the week. For more information about the Casino Showboat, you can call the Parkville Chamber of Commerce at (816) 587–2700.

If you are a devotee of fine baked good, you'll want—no, you'll *need*—to stop by **Fannie's Restaurant** in Platte City (816–431–5675), just across from the recently restored courthouse. Fannie's can serve 150 hungry diners at once, and it's a good thing; busloads of young recruits from Ft. Leavenworth, Kansas, just across the Missouri River, make the trek to taste the cooking that reminds them of home. Homemade bread comes with the meal, or you can buy a giant, fluffy loaf to take home; try the pies, cinnamon rolls, and cobblers as well. Oh, yes, the meals are fine, too. They run from $6.75 to $10.95, or enjoy the smorgasbord on Tuesday, Wednesday, and Thursday—all you can eat for $6.95. Fannie's also features lots of preserves, relishes, and fresh spices from the Amish in Jamesport; buy a jar of apple butter to serve on that warm bread.

Just off Highway 45, Weston is a beautiful town tucked between rounded loess hills, its past shaped as much by the nearby Missouri River and its thread of commerce as by the vineyards, distilleries, and good tobacco-growing soils here. It must have seemed like the perfect place for a town, and it still is. After the signing of the 1837 Platte Purchase, it attracted settlers who recognized its rich soils—and appreciated the low prices.

Historic preservation in Weston has been a high priority for many years; the place exudes charm like a flower exudes scent. A beautiful old Catholic church overlooks the town, and tobacco and apple barns stand tall on many of the surrounding hills. It has a foursquare flavor that just feels historic—and in fact, Weston bills itself as the Midwest's most historic town. There are over 200 historically significant homes and businesses from before the Civil War alone. Book a tour of the homes (advance reservations are required for the tour; call (816) 386–5235) or visit the Weston Museum at Main and Spring streets. Life in Platte County goes way back, long before these neat homes were built or the first still was cranked up; the museum will take you from prehistoric times through World War II. The hours are from 1:00 P.M. till 4:00 P.M. Tuesday through Saturday and Sunday from 1:30 P.M. till 5:00 P.M. This one is a bargain; admission is free. Call (816) 386–2650 or –2977. It's a day trip all by itself.

Missouri has more than its share of fine little wineries, and several world-class breweries, from giant Anheuser-Busch to Kansas City's new microbrewery, Boulevard Brewery, where owner/brewmaster John McDonald specializes in Boulevard Pale Ale, an import-style beer. But distilleries (since Prohibition, anyway, when they were all moonshiners) are few and far between. Weston's ⊃**McCormick Distilling Company** (816–386–2276) is a rare treat, 1¼ miles south of town on Highway JJ. They say this is the oldest continuously active distillery in the country—or at least west of the Hudson River. It was founded in 1856 by stagecoach and Pony Express king Ben Holladay (no, not Doc).

Enjoy the fine aroma of strong drink and smokey oaken barrels as you tour the distillery from March through mid-December, Monday through Friday from 9:30 A.M. to 4:00 P.M. or Sunday from 11:00 A.M. till 4:00 P.M. The tour takes about a half hour, and in summer it draws hundreds. The "Ancient Cave" was dug by old Ben himself to store and age his fine product; it's still open to visitors, and in the sultry summer months it's a welcome respite from Missouri heat. The Country Store is open year round; you can pick up McCormick souvenirs or a gift bottle Monday through Saturday from 9:00 A.M. till 5:00 P.M. or Sundays from 10:30 A.M. till 4:00 P.M. Tours are free. Watch those speed bumps on the way in.

Pirtle's Weston Vineyards Winery (816–375–5728 or –5588) is one of Missouri's most interesting wineries, located in the former German Lutheran Evangelical Church at 502 Spring Street. Jesus made wine, why not Pirtle's? Owner Elbert Pirtle's striking new stained-glass windows depict the winery's logo and a wild rose—the math professor from the University of Missouri at Kansas City is quite the Renaissance man.

Northern Platte County soils are conducive to some fine viticulture; taste the products of these rolling hills Monday through Saturday from 10:00 A.M. to 6:00 P.M. and Sunday noon to 6:00 P.M. The Pirtles love to talk wine and vines. Schedule a wine-tasting party here, and don't forget the mead, a honey-based beverage once thought to be a "love potion." (So what have you got to lose?) It's sweet and smokey—and so it should be, since it's aged in McCormick Distillery oak barrels. They say that originally the church was upstairs and a cooperage was in the basement, where barrels were made to serve northwest Missouri.

Across the street at 505 Spring you'll find ⊃**The Vineyards** (816–386–2835). It's a restaurant featuring continental cuisine and is considered one of the finest places to eat in the Kansas City area. With that reputation, you'd best call for reservations; the place is charming but small, seating only thirty-six . . . well, forty-two in a pinch, if they push the tables together. The kitchen is tucked into every nook and cranny in the basement. Patio dining during fine weather is a treat. There's a nice mix of art and music in the tiny 1845 Rumpel House.

Just around the corner northwest from the Vineyards is the **American Bowman Restaurant** ("where the Past is Present"), the oldest continuously operating pub in Weston at 150 rollicking years old. It offers Irish-style food and entertainment, pewter mugs and kerosene lamps on the tables; there's O'Malley's 1842 Pub, the Post Ordinary, the Heritage Theater, and malt and hops cellars in the same building (as well as an antiques mall).

At Christmas, try the Dickens Dinner; at other seasons, 1837 Dinners, Civil War Dinners, and 19th Century Irish Banquets are yours for the ordering. For reservations call (816) 386–5235.

Steamboat Gothic describes Ken and Karen West's place, the **Benner House Bed and Breakfast** (816–386–2616) at 645 Main Street. With its double-deck, wraparound porch and gingerbread trim, the jaunty, turn-of-the-century mansion looks as if it could steam away like the nearby riverboats. Brass beds, baths with pullchain water closets, and claw-foot tubs add to the interior decor and to your mood. Ken whisks guests around town in his 1929 Ford Phaeton touring car and Karen's candlelit breakfasts star cinnamon twists and apple-puff pancakes. A double room is $65.

If you are in the mood to taste a batch of unusual gourmet items, climb the stairs to Benzinger's, a charming kitchen and gourmet shop above an antiques shop at 415 Main Street. Imagine cream cheese and hot/sweet jalapeños on crackers, praline sauce to coat a chicken breast, pumpkin butter, raspberry jam, and an amazing collection of beautiful herb vinegars. Helen will let you try (actually insist you try) anything that catches your interest. Call (816) 386–2222. Like most places in Weston, it is closed on Monday. Mettier Hall, on the third floor of a historic downtown building, hosts kitchen music concerts (dinner and entertainment) and an occasional appearance by Seartaglen, an Irish-music group winning a national reputation.

Weston Antique Center is only one of many great places to shop here; there are two floors of goodies in three old storefronts, open from 10:00 A.M. to 5:00 P.M. weekdays, 10:00 A.M. to 6:00 P.M. Saturday, and noon to 5:00 P.M. Sunday.

And just across the street and catty-corner to the west is an old white building that looks like a tiny old-fashioned service station. That's because it *was* in a previous incarnation. Now it's **Diddy-Wa-Diddy,** a great and wacky place full of funky sculpture, gifts, pillows, and other goodies. There's no phone number, so you'll have to catch as catch can—but do catch, the Diddy's worth it for irresistible, one-of-a-kind buys. This is no goose-with-a-raffia-bow place!

If history is your love—and the name Daniel Boone rings a bell—be sure to visit the **Price-Loyles House and Blackhawk Trading Company** just north of Main Street at 718 Spring (816–386–2383). This tidy brick home belonged in the Boone family from 1857 to 1989, and all original family furnishings and historic documents were carefully restored and preserved by the present owners. Interestingly, it was mostly the women of the Boone family who owned the home, passing it down from mother to daughter; their delightful furnishings reflect a century and a half of living, but with never a formica-and-chrome era to be found. They appreciated their heritage and held on to it. You will see the original Victorian beds and clothing, books, the children's room, the old piano—in short, the place looks as if you'd just come to call on a lovely day in the 1800s.

Blackhawk Trading Company is a fine antiques and gift store on the lower level of the home, where you enter to take a tour; admission to the house is $3.50 per person, with discounts for senior citizens, students, and groups.

Take a short jaunt west of Weston back on Highway 45 to see a view worth going *way* out of your way for. **Weston Bend State Park** is one of Missouri's newest, and the scenic overlook that spreads a panorama of the Missouri River and rolling fields, wooded loess hills, and Leavenworth clear across the river in Kansas is simply not to be missed. There's also camping, picnicking, hiking, and bicycling, if that's your pleasure.

A bit farther west and almost to the bridge to Kansas is the **Beverly Hills Antiques Mall**—definitely *not* in California. Sure, there are plenty of antiques malls across the state, some better than others. This one's one of the best, with high-quality goods and plenty of variety from fifty-five dealers. No garage sale stuff here, thank you. The mall is open Tuesday through Saturday from 10:00 A.M. to 5:00 P.M. You can't miss it; it's in the old

133

two-story Beverly Lumber Company building, and there's virtually nothing else there—but if you get lost, call (816) 546–3432 and they'll send out the Mounties.

Snow Creek Ski Area (816–386–2200), just north of Weston, is open seven days a week through the cold months. There's plenty of manmade snow (up to 4 feet), lifts, a ski rental, and a cozy lodge for *après ski*. Normal costs including equipment rental run $34. (Yes, there *is* downhill skiing in Missouri; the big hills near the Missouri River are satisfyingly steep, if not long. You can still break a leg if you're so inclined.)

Iatan Marsh near the water treatment plant is the place to be in winter if you're a birder. The warmer waters here attract flocks of migrant waterfowl; who knows what you might spot in December.

Nearby Bean Lake and Little Bean Marsh catch the birds—and birders—year round. You may see rails and bitterns, yellow-headed blackbirds, green herons, and egrets along with the ducks and geese. An observation tower makes sighting easier; Little Bean Marsh is the largest remaining natural marsh in Missouri, a remnant of our wetlands heritage.

If you've read Lewis and Clark's journals, you'll remember the description of an oxbow they dubbed "Gosling Lake." This is now thought to be Sugar Lake in Lewis and Clark State Park (816–579–5564), just off Highway 59. There's a huge fish hatchery here; you can see anything from fry to fingerlings to lunkers.

St. Joseph is a river town that lost the race to Kansas City when K.C. was first to bridge the Muddy Mo with the Hannibal Bridge. Still a big and bustling town, it has plenty for the day-tripper to do and see. Consider this: St. Joe has eight, count 'em, eight, museums. The ⊃**Albrecht Art Museum** (816–233–7003) has a collection of some of the finest American art in the country, including works by Mary Cassatt, William Merritt Chase, George Catlin, and Missouri's own Thomas Hart Benton. Housed in an old Georgian manse, the museum at 2818 Frederick has been in operation since 1966. Hours are Tuesday through Friday from 10:00 A.M. to 4:00 P.M. and weekends from 1:00 P.M. to 4:00 P.M.. Admission is free.

Then of course there's 1858 Patee House (St. Joseph's only National Historic Landmark and a magnificent old hotel that was the original headquarters for the Pony Express) and the Jesse James Museum (816–232–8206). Roubidoux Row; and the Doll

Museum. **The Pony Express Museum** at 914 Penn Street chronicles the history of these early mail runs. Check it out for little more than the price of a stamp ($1.00 for adults and 50 cents for children), April through October from 9:00 A.M. to 5:00 P.M.

There's a morbid fascination to this next one, the ⊃**St. Joseph Hospital Psychiatric Museum** (816–387–2300). The museum is housed in an old, rather forbidding wing on the hospital grounds at 3400 Frederick. If you get a little shaky mentally, consider yourself fortunate that it's the 1990s; the museum features twenty display rooms of arcane treatments for psychiatric disorders, from prehistoric times to the recent past. (What did cave men do, you ask? Knocked a hole in your skull to let out the evil spirits. Some patients even lived!) The museum is handicapped accessible, and admission is free.

Missing a museum? It's the St. Joseph Museum at Eleventh and Charles streets, founded in 1926. Enjoy displays of North American Indian crafts and Midwestern wildlife as well as the trading post exhibit.

Get yourself a ten-gallon hat (or a nice cap) at the **Stetson Hat Outlet** (816–233–3286), 4500 Stetson Trail just off Interstate 29 and exit 44. Hours are 8:00 A.M. to 4:30 P.M. Monday through Saturday. These guys have been in business since 1857, so they know hats.

Harding House Bed and Breakfast at 219 North Twentieth Street is a gracious turn-of-the-century home with beveled-glass windows, oak woodwork, and many antiques. Hosts Glen and Mary Harding serve tea or sherry by the fire in cool weather and on the porch during the warm months. There's a full American breakfast, topped off with homemade pastries. Rates are from $30 to $35 for a single and from $35 to $40 for a double; each additional person is $10. One grand room has a queen-size bed and rents for $55. For reservations call the B&B service at (314) 965–4328.

Jerre Anne Cafeteria and Bakery (816–232–6585) has whipped up home-style cooking since 1930; they're *good* at it. Everything is their specialty—everything they sell here, they make here. Try the gooseberry pie or the fruit salad pie, originated in the thirties and still sold today to an enthusiastic clientele. The chicken and dumplings is better that Grandma's, and the pork tenderloin is breaded and fried to perfection. They also do a brisk carryout business; the apricot nut bread is wonderful.

Jerre Anne's is open Tuesday through Saturday from 11:00 A.M. to 7:00 P.M. and Sunday from 11:00 A.M. to 1:30 P.M. at 2640 Mitchell Avenue.

For sheer spectacle, visit ⊃**Squaw Creek National Wildlife Refuge** (816–442–3187) during the fall migration. You may see up to 350,000 snow geese filling the air like clouds—but these clouds are full of thunder. The sound of that many wings is deafening. Show, blue, and Canada geese, migrating ducks and attendant bald eagles (as many as 150 representatives of our national symbol) plus coyotes, beavers, muskrats, and deer make this a wildlife-lover's paradise. At least 268 species of birds have been recorded on the refuge. It's an essential stop on the flyway for migratory waterfowl and it has been for centuries; this area was described in the journals of Lewis and Clark. There are now 7,193 acres on the refuge just off Highway 159; watch for signs. Unusual loess hills that look like great dunes, reddish and fantastically eroded, are threaded with hiking trails. Spring redbud season is gorgeous here.

Squaw Creek National Wildlife Refuge

If all this excitement makes you hungry, rangers at Squaw Creek suggest the **Forest City Diner** at tiny Forest City, 6 or 7 miles from the refuge on Highway 111. You can only get breakfast and lunch here—might as well make it the homemade pie.

Big Lake State Park near Mound City is the largest natural lake in this state of manmade lakes, a 615-acre oxbow remnant of the Missouri River channel. Camping is available here, which is handy if you want to stay near Squaw Creek.

Maryville is a college town, home of Northwest Missouri State University. It is also home to a gaggle of little antiques shops and malls. Visit **Memory Lane Antique Mall** at 316 East Third (816–582–5990); 71 Antiques at 523 North Main (816–562–2899); or Five Mile Corner Antique Mall on Highway 71 South. There's more to do here than just shop, of course. For instance, you can visit the Mary Linn Performing Arts Theater to hear a concert or watch a play performed by the Missouri Repertory Company.

If all this antiques hunting has you ready for a bit of quiet, retreat from the world at ‚**Conception Abbey** in Conception Junction. Benedictine monks run The Printery House (816–944–2218), where they make greeting cards and colorful notes (ask for their catalog) when they are not going about their real work. Benedictines consider their true work to be prayer—but the work of their hands is prayer, too. Stay over at the 1,000-acre retreat, 900 of which is productive farmland; visit with "the weather monk," or learn along with the seminarians. Call (816) 944–2211 to make a reservation.

As you near Lathrop, your sweet tooth will begin to ache. It's ‚**Candyman's Mule Barn** (816–528–4263), 600 feet off Interstate 35 at the Lathrop exit. An odd name for a candy place, you say? Owners David and Joan Gessert built their new shop to resemble one of the mule barns that put Lathrop on the map; the town was once the mule capital of America, selling hundreds of these sturdy animals at the turn of the century. Foreign buyers flocked to Lathrop, and nearly all the pack animals for the Boer War were from this little Missouri town. All the barns are gone now, and there's no trace of the busy hotels that housed the buyers; so the Gesserts decided to recreate a bit of history.

Joan's dad started the candy factory more than twenty-five years ago, making the best hand-dipped chocolates to come down the pike. The Gesserts do the same; you can watch the kitchen-fresh candy being made daily from 9:00 A.M. to 6:00 P.M.

Hours are the same on weekends, but the candy makers get to go home; you'll have to buy without watching. The gift shop also handles other "Best of Missouri Hands" products, including hillbilly bean soup.

If you like the nostalgic feeling of an old-fashioned, wood-floored variety store—the family-style precursor of today's discount giants—you'll love **McCullough Variety** at 619 Oak Street in Lathrop (816–528–3612). As owners Regina and Donald Moore say, "You name it, we have it."

Shirley and John Grant's Curiosity Corner (816–539–2666) specializes in silver, coins, tools, and furniture at 216 North Main. Tiques & Stuff (816–539–3232) is Charles and Michele Spease's place on the east side of the courthouse. It is open Monday through Saturday from 10:00 A.M. to 5:00 P.M.

A quick detour up Highway 169 will take you to Gower; doll collectors, be alerted. Janice Hall, owner of **Hall's of Yesteryear** (302 Railroad Avenue, 816–424–6208), collects small French and German bisque dolls, composition Shirley Temples, international dolls, paper dolls, old toys, doll furniture, vintage clothing—anything your heart desires. "I try to offer a wide variety," says Janice, "including doll umbrellas, furnishings, dishes—anything you'd have found in an old-fashioned playroom." Janice's babies are often found at shows and malls, including the new Interstate–29 Antiques Mall in Platte City, but the shop is where you'll find her in the warmer months. Janice's is open by appointment, so do call ahead.

Smithville is near the intersection of Highways 169 and 92, and if all you know about the place is that it used to flood, you're in for a nice surprise. The town is close by the new Smithville Lake for summer fun, and there are plenty of shops to browse.

The **Bowry Soda Shoppe** (816–873–3212) at 100 South Bridge is an "olde tyme soda shoppe" to help cool down those hot summer days. This shoppe is in a hundred-year-old bank building. Owners Elbert and Nancy Pigg saw the tin ceilings, octagonal-tiled floors, and a fat, round seven-ton safe and thought it would make the perfect soda fountain. It did.

The old-fashioned lights, jukebox, framed photos of early Smithville (including one of the bank when it was still a bank), and ceiling fans help set the mood, and real carbonated fountain drinks are created right before your eyes. They even serve an esoteric concoction called "Green River"; if you remember what that is, you'll remember the charm of soda fountains like this one. The vault serves as a storeroom, keeping the goodies safe from intruders. They serve soup and sandwiches, too. Summer hours are 10:00 A.M. to 10:00 P.M. except Monday; winter hours are 11:00 A.M. to 3:00 P.M.

‚**Smithville Lake** is a fairly recent addition to Missouri's array of manmade lakes. Constructed by the Corps of Engineers to control flooding that Smithville residents have lived with since there was a Smithville, the lake is also a magnet for water-lovers. Turn north off Highway 92 (between Kearney and the town of Smithville) for sailing, fishing, boating, or just messing around.

You'll find waterfowl by the thousands in season; you may even spot a bald eagle or two in the winter. Honker Cove Waterfowl Refuge is on a protected arm of the lake; it's closed to boating (not to mention fishing, hunting, or trapping) during the busiest migration seasons, from October to mid-January.

Also at the lake is Missouri's own Woodhenge, a re-creation of a Woodland Indian site that may have been used as an astronomical observatory around 5,000 years ago. The original location of Woodhenge was uncovered during the building of the lake, and dredging was halted until archaeologists could study the area. It was important enough that the present site was reconstructed as an aid to further study; scientists from Woods Hole, Massachusetts, have come here to observe the solstice and equinox.

Near the new dam at Smithville Lake one of the largest glacial erratics in the area squats like a patient dinosaur under an accretion of graffiti. A large, pink Sioux-quartzite stone, this elephant-sized monster was brought here by the last glacier some 15,000 years ago. It may have been an important landmark for the Paleo-Indians who live in the area.

At the Jerry Litton Visitors' Center (816–532–0174), also near the dam, you can find out about these earliest inhabitants, about visits by Lewis and Clark as they came through on the nearby Missouri River, about the pioneer settlers, and about the birds and animals that make this area home. Admission is free.

About 3½ miles north of Smithville on Highway 169, you can turn right on Highway W and drive 2 miles across the east side of the lake to Paradise. This community is home to about twenty-five families and Ed Gilliam, a man who carves Father Christmas, some sixty-seven styles of Santas, and, coincidentally, looks as though he should be surrounded by elves himself. Perhaps it is because he was born on Christmas Day. Ed has been carving since he was twelve years old—that's over fifty years now—and still fills his shop with piles of Missouri and Minnesota basswood, sugar pine, cottonwood bark, and driftwood bits that drop from the hundreds of carvings lining the shop. Santas of every style line the walls. There are fat Santas and thin Santas, Black Santas and Uncle Sam Santas. Or how about a German Belznickle, a rather stern-looking Santa who carries a switch.

They are not all Santas, though. Ed turns out cigar store Indians, folk art, cowboys, and all manner of Americana ranging from four inches to four feet in height. Ed is usually at his house in Paradise or in the shop down on Main Street in Smithville, but it would be a good idea to call first, (816) 873–2592. To find Ed's house find Clyde's General Store, a two-story brick building, then turn right at the end of the building and go two blocks to Holmes Street. Ed's place is at 18403 Holmes Street.

Off the Beaten Path in Northeast Missouri

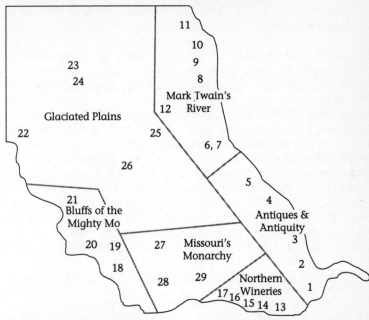

1. *Spirit of St. Charles* Riverboat
2. Red Lantern Antiques
3. Lock and Dam No. 25
4. Apple Shed Cultural Center
5. Orthwein Mansion Bed and Breakfast
6. Ayers Pottery
7. Garth Woodside Mansion
8. Golden Eagle Riverboat Dinner Theatre
9. St. Patrick
10. Sheffler Rock Shop and Geode Mine
11. Battle of Athens State Park
12. Bethel
13. Daniel Boone's Home
14. Mount Pleasant Wine Company
15. Nona Woodworks
16. Blumenhof Vineyards and Winery
17. Concord Hill Bed and Breakfast
18. Rock Bridge State Park
19. Museum of Art and Archaeology
20. Moniteau Creek Pottery
21. Henderson's
22. General John J. Pershing Boyhood Home
23. Andrew Taylor Still National Osteopathic Museum
24. Thousand Hills State Park
25. Mark Twain Birthplace State Historic Site
26. Chance Gardens
27. Kingdom of Callaway
28. Winston Churchill Memorial and Library
29. Graham Cave State Park

Northeast Missouri

North of St. Louis, the land changes. Hills are gentler—the legacy of a wall of glacial ice that smoothed rough edges and brought with it tons of rich, deep soil some 15,000 years ago. Thanks to that gift, quintessentially Mid-American towns are dotted with the docile shapes of cows; barns are large and prosperous-looking; fence rows blossom with wildflowers; and bluebirds and meadowlarks sing.

Northeast Missouri is rich in history as well. That consummate storyteller Mark Twain was born here; he has endowed us with more colorful quotes than any writer before or since. You've heard of Mark Twain Cave and his boyhood home in Hannibal, but did you know that near Florida, Missouri, you can explore Samuel Clemens's birthplace? General Omar Bradley's birthplace is in this area, too, along with General John J. Pershing's boyhood home and a monument to General Sterling Price. (Generally speaking, it seems to be a great place for great men.)

The Civil War raged from St. Louis to the Iowa border, where the Battle of Athens took place. Tiny Palmyra was the site of an atrocity that presidents Abraham Lincoln and Jefferson Davis called the worst of war crimes.

All along the Missouri River valley are tiny, picturesque towns, many with a German heritage—and many with wineries where you may taste the best the United States has to offer (Mt. Pleasant's Port won the gold in international competition). Lewis and Clark passed by these town sites on their way to the Northwest Passage and remarked on them in their journals.

The mighty Mississippi is busy with commerce, as it has been for over 200 years. Barges churn by, and the power of that mile-wide channel vibrates under you as you stand on a riverboat's deck. The Great River Road, which runs along the Mississippi from New Orleans to the source, is so picturesque that plans are afoot to make it a National Scenic Roadway.

Bald eagles feed along both rivers in winter, drawn by open water and good fishing below the locks and dams. Amish communities, college towns, museums, eateries, petroglyphs, wildlife refuges—whatever your interest, you'll find it satisfied in northeast Missouri, where literally everything is off the beaten path.

Antiques and Antiquity

Just north of St. Louis is St. Charles. The first capitol of Missouri is located at 208–216 South Main Street (314–946–9282); legislators met here until October 1826, when the abandoned buildings began to settle slowly into decay. In 1961 the state of Missouri began a ten-year restoration project that sparked the revitalization of St. Charles. Shops, restaurants, and delightful little surprises abound. Take a walking tour of history; the St. Charles Convention and Visitors' Bureau (314–946–7776) can get you started.

If your sweet tooth kicks in and you've a dime or two in your pocket, satisfy that craving the old-fashioned way at **Pop's General Store,** 322 South Main (314–723–6040). Imagine an old-style emporium with a potbellied stove, brass cash register, and advertising memorabilia from soap powders to nostrums; that place is here. Richard House (otherwise known as Pop) sacks horehound candy, peppermint drops, and other old favorites by the pound or by the piece.

With your sweet tooth satisfied, you can take a daytime, dinner, or moonlight cruise on the ⊃*Spirit of St. Charles* **Riverboat,** moored at the foot of First Capitol Drive at the Missouri River.

Both of our big rivers claimed more than their share of casualties. Steamboats sank with dismal regularity, and to this day—locks and dams notwithstanding—riverboat captains watch their charts and take their soundings much as Samuel Clemens did when he sang out, "Mark twain." The channels of both the Missouri and the Mississippi are graveyards for boats from tugs to stern-wheelers; the rivers are not to be taken lightly. Our Lady of the Rivers shrine, a lighthouselike monument at Portage de Sioux, is a reminder that brave travelers needed all the help they could get.

Old Monroe, Winfield, Foley, Clarksville, Louisiana—the names are strung like beads along the Great River Road (now Highway 79) between St. Louis and Hannibal. These little towns harbor more antiques shops than you know what to do with. There are so many, in fact, that we only have room to include those towns that have additional attractions. Don't let that stop you, though; Missouri is a mecca for affordable goodies. If you can't find what you're looking for, you just haven't found the magic spot yet, and isn't the search as much fun as the finding?

143

Old Monroe is 14 miles up from the pike from St. Charles. ↄ**Red Lantern Antiques** (314–665–5114), one block north of the stop sign on Highway 79, shines on furniture, collectibles, and primitives. Catch owners Jim and Carol Russell at their shop from 9:00 A.M. to 5:00 P.M.

ↄ**Lock and Dam No. 25** on the Mississippi is a fine place to watch the eagles feed in the winter. Or take the old Winfield Ferry across the river to Calhoon County, Illinois. (Don't worry, you can come right back if you're not through antiques hunting.)

If you fancy a bit of wilderness about now, a short detour west on Highway 47 will take you to spectacular Cuivre River State Park (314–528–7247). More than 31 miles of trails will let you discover one of the state's most rustic parks. The rough terrain is more like the Ozarks than the rest of glacier-smoothed northern Missouri, and like the Ozarks, it encourages many plants only found farther south—flowering dogwood, Missouri orange coneflower, and dittany, among others. Frenchman's Bluff overlooks the Cuivre River Valley. The Lincoln Hills region, where Cuivre River State Park is found, formed millions of years ago when intense pressures caused the earth to buckle. Erosion cut even deeper; the resulting springs, sinkholes, and rocky cliffs make this an outdoor-lover's paradise. Archaeologists speculate that the region was home to prehistoric humans as early as 12,000 years ago; a 1937 dig unearthed a stone chamber containing a skeleton and pieces of a clay pot.

Clarksville is finding its way back—toward the past. With about the same population that it had in 1860, this spic-and-span town has new life in its old veins. A historic preservation effort mounted in 1987 has saved many of the delightful buildings in record time. One of those buildings is the Clifford Banking Company, now an antiques store, where you'll find furniture and accessories from 10:00 A.M. to 5:00 P.M. most days. Next door is the Front Street Gallery, a co-op composed of artists from St. Charles to the Hannibal area. Other downtown commercial buildings, homes, and churches have already been restored, and more are on the way. Plenty of other antiques stores are nearby; ask at Clifford's.

The **Clifford Wirick Centennial House** at 105 South Second Street (314–242–3376) is on the National Register of Historic Places. If you love stained glass—old or new—you'll find this place to your liking. They also do repairs if you have a favorite piece that needs attention. Owner/historian Vernon Hughes will be here to answer your questions about Clarksville or provide you with fine examples of American dinnerware, glass, china, pottery, and prints. The house is open from 10:00 A.M. till 5:00 P.M. most days.

The town commands an 800-square-mile view of the valley of the Big Muddy from an aerie on the highest point overlooking the Mississippi. Surprisingly, barge traffic on the river below is constant—you don't expect to see so much action. See ice-formed drumlins (those are hills) in this panoramic view from Look-Out Point, 600 feet above the river. This is one place you probably won't want to walk. Take the skylift; the charge is $5.00 for adults, and children five to twelve ride for $3.00.

Up top, check out the country store; you'll find folk art, country cooking, home-style candy, and souvenirs. The kids can let off some of the steam they've built up in the back of the van all day. There are a jungle gym, video games, and a wonderful tilted house.

Clarksville is a great place to observe wintering eagles; the Missouri Department of Conservation's Eagle Days, held here the last weekend of January, can swell the town's normal population of 500 to over 5,000. Is it worth it? You bet it is. Even the *New York Times* visited to check out the 340 to 350 bald eagles. The Great River Road Visitors' Center offers information, a museum, and spanking-clean restrooms. The ⊃**Apple Shed Cultural Center** hosts various festivals including a fine arts festival; in addition, the Opera Theatre of St. Louis presents opera here at least once a year.

In Louisiana, you'll come face to face with temptation—if you're an antiques nut, that is. **Jeanne's House of Antiques** (314–754–6836), one block east of the highway on Virginia Street, is open every day from 10:00 A.M. to 5:00 P.M. There are twenty rooms stuffed with everything from china and silver (you could set an elegant, although eclectic, table from your finds) to lovely old quilts, stoneware, primitives, and crafts. The building's a kick, too. It's a huge mansion with a wraparound porch and big windows that let in the light.

While you're in Louisiana, visit **Steamboat Classics Antiques** at 300 North Main, with their selection of Victoriana, vintage clothing, old lace, paper, and prints—all sorts of ephemera. There's even a bride's room if you want to put on a period wedding. Make reservations for tours or lunch in their tea room by calling (314) 754–3243. Steamboat Classics is open weekends from 10:00 A.M. to 5:00 P.M. and weekdays by appointment.

It's not all just antiques and eats in Louisiana; if you're a history buff, you'll enjoy the Georgia Street Historic District, where the ⊃**Orthwein Mansion Bed and Breakfast,** a baronial manse, offers pure class. It was featured in *Midwest Living, St. Louis* magazine, and *Ozark Airlines* magazine. Reservations are made through River Country Bed and Breakfast, (314) 771–1993.

Mark Twain's River

For tourists, Hannibal is not exactly "off the beaten path." Half a million people annually come through this picturesque little town. Everybody knows about the Mark Twain Boyhood Home. Everybody's seen that fence—or at least pictures of it—where Tom Sawyer tricked his buddies into doing his work for him. (The original fence was nine feet tall and a *lot* longer than the one that stands here now—no *wonder* the kid didn't want to paint it by himself.) You may even know about Margaret Tobin Brown's home (remember the Unsinkable Molly Brown?), the Molly Brown Dinner Theater, and the fine dinner cruise on the Mississippi riverboat, the *Mark Twain*. So we'll let you find them on your own—it's easy.

While you're in the historic district, though, look for ⊃**Ayers Pottery.** Steve Ayers does beautiful work, primarily using Missouri clays, and the shop is set up to encourage your involvement. There's a hall around three sides of the workshop, so you can see every step in the process. He also stocks a selection of beautiful kites, porcelain jewelry, baskets, and handforged things—goodies he picks up while on the craft-show circuit.

Even if Steve's out of town, the shop will be open at 308 North Third, seven days a week in the summer from 8:00 A.M. to 5:00 P.M. (314–221–6960). It's only a half-block from the Mark Twain Museum.

If elegant Victoriana is your weakness, stay in gingerbread heaven at the ⊃**Garth Woodside Mansion.** This one's on the National Register, and it deserves to be. Mark Twain was often a guest of the Garths.

You won't believe the three-story flying staircase with no visible means of support; you might not trust it, either, though they

Garth Woodside Mansion

say it's quite safe. Enter the walnut-lined library through 9-foot doors, or check out the extra-wide hostess's seat in the dining room (no, the hostess wasn't that wide; it accommodated the voluminous petticoats of the era). Rates are from $58 to $95. Call (314) 221-2789.

If you prefer to visit instead of staying over, tour the common rooms, from 11:30 A.M. to 3:00 P.M. every day from Memorial Day to Labor Day. (Off-season, you'd best call ahead.) Innkeepers Irv and Diane Feinberg go all out. For large tour groups they will arrange a tea and tour, complete with hot or iced tea (according to season) and Victorian-style goodies. The mansion is in a beautiful country setting—thirty-nine acres of meadows and woodlands that retain the feel of early Hannibal countryside.

Don't miss the mansion where Mr. Clemens addressed the cream of Hannibal society on his last visit here in 1902. It's **Rockcliffe Mansion** (314–221–4140), at 1000 Bird Street, a wonderfully quirky place full of Art Nouveau decor, which was a breakaway style from the established Victorian. It, too, is on the National Register of Historic Places.

There are guided tours daily from March through November, 9:30 A.M. till 5:00 P.M., and from December through February, 11:30 A.M. till 3:30 P.M. There's a $4.00 charge for adults, and kids six through eleven can see the place for $1.50.

If all this running around makes you hungry, drop in to the Mark Twain Family Restaurant, right next to the Twain Home at Third and Hill streets. It's Hannibal's hometown restaurant (that's what they say, really). Listen up—you may overhear the tall tales from the Liar's Table; get good enough, and maybe you'll earn a place there. They're famous for their tenderloins and onion rings, but if you've never had a Maid Rite, try one. A good portion of the American public grew up on these weird little burgers! Dinner's a bit more serious, with fried chicken, charbroiled steaks, and seafood. Prices are modest, and the place is open from 6:00 A.M. till 10:00 P.M.

The path to Mark Twain Cave is pretty well beaten smooth, but nearby Cameron Cave (314–221–1656) is closer to the underground experience of Huck and Injun Joe. Here, instead of a fully electrified, ride-through cave, you'll find a complex, mazelike place where folks still carry lanterns. Don't worry, though; the tour meets all state safety requirements. It's Missouri's newest showcave, Memorial Day through Labor Day. The cost is $8.50 for adults, $5.50 for children eight to twelve; if you tour Mark Twain Cave on the same weekend, you'll receive a discount.

Driving past Palmyra's sleepy storefronts, you may not guess the colorful history—and the pain—these buildings have seen. Even tiny, northern Palmyra wasn't exempt from the horrors of the Civil War; a few Union troops were garrisoned here, but the town itself held largely southern sympathies. The Union held a few southern prisoners, but by and large exchanges were polite—pleasant, almost—until October 8, 1862. On that day, ten young Confederates—all local boys—were paraded down Main Street before townspeople and kin to face thirty muskets of the Second Missouri State Militia. Only three were killed outright; a second squad was called in to finish the job with pistols. The boys were executed when Confederate Colonel John C. Porter couldn't—or wouldn't—return a captured pro-Union civilian. The event is a harsh reminder of wartime ethics and of retaliation of the worst kind. Both President Lincoln and Jefferson Davis called the Palmyra Massacre the "darkest crime of the Civil War."

The "Robin Hood of the Thirties," John Dillinger often made Palmyra an overnight stop between Chicago and Kansas City. Lucky Palmyra; his "overnights" included a kidnapping and a bank robbery.

There are over 200 pre–Civil War buildings here, many of them restored. Architecture buffs can watch for these styles: Federal (1800–1840); Greek Revival (1820–1860); Gothic (1840–1860); Italianate (1840–1885); Eastlake (1870–1890); Queen Anne (1875–1900); Romanesque (1870–1900); and Prairie (1900–1920). It's an old-house lover's dream. The staff at the Visitor's Information Center in the Civil War Museum and Gift Shop can steer you to what you want to see.

There's an antiques store or two hidden in old Palmyra; scout around. Perhaps you'll find one on a Friday morning in June, July, or August when you stop by the local farmers market for fresh produce and baked goods.

Look . . . there, by the side of the road. A riverboat's run aground! Well, not really, but it sure looks that way. The ⊃**Golden Eagle Riverboat Dinner Theatre** (314–288–5273) at Canton was built where she sits, firmly at anchor in Missouri's rich, alluvial soil. It's one of the state's most unusual businesses, to say the least. It will put you in mind of the old diners shaped like a coffeepot or a hot dog (at the risk of sounding irreverent).

This landlocked beauty inside the Canton levee at Second and Green streets incorporates many authentic bits of riverboat memorabilia. The Grand Salon is modeled after the finest old packets ever to steam up the Muddy Mississip.

Don't miss the live entertainment. There are musical comedies, melodramas, and vaudeville reviews featuring members of the Showboat Company. And just because this eagle is landlocked doesn't mean there's no calliope. The sound of a steam calliope seems wedded to these steam-powered boats, since the music was powered by the same hot vapor that drove the engines. Owner and producer Captain Dave Steinbeck puts on one heck of a concert each evening during the summer months.

If you've just *got* to get out on that river, the Canton Ferry, owned by Mr. and Mrs. Wallace Kiser, will whisk you over and back. There's been a ferry in continuous operation here since 1853.

If you're at all Irish (and who isn't, at least one day of the year), don't miss ⊃**St. Patrick,** the only town in the world (with a post office) named for everybody's patron saint. If you like, send a package of mail containing stamped, addressed envelopes to Postmaster Harriet Johnson, St. Patrick, MO 63466, to get the special St. Paddy's Day cancellation.

It's more fun to visit the post office, though. The letter boxes are antique, and the hospitality is the old-fashioned kind you'd expect in a town of twenty-three souls. Hours are 9:00 A.M. till 1:00 P.M.

The **Old Irish Antiques and Gift Shop** is in the John N. Kirchner store building, the oldest building standing in St. Patrick today. It once housed the general store and post office; today the Kirchner grandchildren run the store, and once again you'll find the post office here. Marcia Hardin and Myrna Daugherty sell antiques, handmade gifts, and souvenirs. They are open seven days a week from 9:00 A.M. to 5:00 P.M.

The Shrine of St. Patrick is fashioned after the Church of Four Masters in Donegal, Ireland; the style is ancient Celtic. There's a round bell tower with a circular staircase of the kind used on the Auld Sod. Dublin-made stained-glass windows are patterned after the famous illuminated manuscript, the *Book of Kells;* the most unusual has St. Patrick surrounded by the symbols of Ireland's four provinces, Ulster, Leinster, Munster, and Connaught. Perhaps you are beginning to catch the flavor of the place.

If you want a real taste of old St. Patrick, drop in the R. C. Logsdon Grocery Store. Laveta Logsdon has owned and operated a general merchandise store here since 1929. You'll like the inventory as much as the atmosphere; Laveta stocks a complete line of groceries, ice cream, sandwiches or cold cuts, hardware, embroidery thread, oil, fishing supplies, film, seed corn—you name it, she has it.

This is a whimsical little town. Mrs. Kenneth Kreuger of the St. Patrick's Information Center (816–754–6028) swore that "leprechaun Jason Richmond was our honorary mayor in 1988" and enclosed a picture of the lad. Seeing is believing, and if you think that smacks of blarney, we hardly know what to tell ye. Each year a new leprechaun—ah, mayor—is chosen, recently one from the green hills of Ireland itself, a good gentleman named Tommy Murphy. Since he is from the Auld Sod, he is a *lifetime* honorary mayor.

Radio station WGEM of nearby Quincy, Illinois, broadcasts live from St. Patrick on March 17; in 1992 the broadcast was carried all over Ireland as well as northeast Missouri and its neighbors.

Oh, yes, there's one other attraction—geodes. What's a geode, you may ask? You must not be a rock hound, if you are wondering. A geode is a rather undistinguished blob that looks like a rounded river rock. But inside—ah, inside, there is *magic*. Beautiful crystal formations fill the hollow center of a geode like a Fabergé egg; they're considered gemstones.

Some of the world's finest geodes are found in this small area. You can buy one at the Old Irish Antique Shop, at Buschling Place 3 miles north of Dempsey; the Buschlings specialize in country crafts, turquoise, and, of course, geodes. Or you can find your own at ⊃**Sheffler Rock Shop and Geode Mine** (816–754–6443), located at the junction of Highway 61 and the Highway 136 Spur, from April to December. This is the only geode mine in the U.S. that is registered with the Federal Bureau of Mines. Watch for the round rock building made entirely of sixty tons of mineral specimens. This shop is open all year round and has been selling minerals, agates, and jewelry-making supplies for more than thirty years. But if you come to dig your own geode, bring a rock hammer and a bit of muscle; these treasures don't come without sweat equity.

Just north of Kahoka is the ⊃**Battle of Athens State Park.** The battlefield at Athens is quiet now; there is only the soft whisper of wind in the trees and the muffled sound of the nearby Des Moines River. On August 5, 1861, that was not the case. The first shots of the opening battle of the Civil War had scarcely died away when the people of Missouri began to take sides. Like it or not, feeling ran strong and families found themselves split down the middle. Groups of men banded together to protect themselves and their kin: Southern sympathizers formed the State Guard Units, Unionists formed the Home Guards, and clashes were inevitable. Visit the park and learn more about the two hours that put this tiny place on history's map.

⊃**Bethel** is the kind of place you dream about when you're feeling nostalgic for "the good old days" when things were simpler and the world was more easily understood, when people could meet one another's eyes directly and a handshake meant everything. Bethel old-timers say, "When you get it right, why change?" And here, they've pulled it off.

It's not all old-time ambience and down-home goodies. Bethel has a thriving art colony. The town plays host to frequent festivals, workshops, and seminars celebrating its agricultural, cultural, and social heritage throughout the year. Thousands of people flock here for the World Sheep and Wool Festival (ouch! a pun!). Other festivals throughout the year draw folks for antiques, fiddlers, music, and Christmas in Bethel. If you see a line on the sidewalk downtown, likely it's for the family storefront bakery that only opens during festivals. Breads, cinnamon rolls—they've got it. Get in line!

Founded as a utopian religious colony in 1844, the whole town is listed on the National Register of Historic Places. The museum can fill you in on the details; it's open daily.

Bethel is friendly; you're family as soon as you arrive. And it's best to arrive hungry. The **Fest Hall Restaurant** (816–284–6493) serves "good food and plenty of it," the folk say, at reasonable family prices. They also serve homemade pies to jettison diets for, seven days a week.

If you want to stay over, the **Bethel German Colony Bed and Breakfast** (same telephone number as Fest Hall) welcomes visitors to four rooms furnished in a simple country style, located above the Colony Restaurant. Incredibly affordable rates of $12.50 per person include a country breakfast blessed with home-baked bread and the Fest Hall's own apple butter. (Close your eyes. Imagine the rich, sweet aroma of bubbling apples and spices in an old copper kettle. That's what goes on your breakfast muffins.) If the restaurant is closed when you arrive, pop over to the grocery store on the corner for room keys.

Northern Wineries

Take a different loop to see the Missouri River and the little wineries that sprout like vines along its banks. There's a lot of history along the Missouri; whatever your interest, you'll find plenty to see and do.

Take Highway 94, for example. It's for people who don't like their roads straight and flat: mile after mile of two-lane blacktop that curves and winds from St. Charles to Jefferson City. It is one of the most beautiful and exhilarating drives in the state and is a practical route to mid-Missouri for those of us who don't enjoy the mind-numbing 65 mph of the interstate. Since you have this book with you, the assumption can be made that you like to drive, so Highway 94 is a "must-do" trip. Cross Interstate 40 outside St. Charles, go a mile, and turn into the **August A. Busch Memorial Wildlife Area.** This 7,000-acre preserve has nature trails, hunting areas, shooting ranges, and thirty-two lakes for fishing. It features a self-guided tour of native prairie, pine plantation, and farming practices that benefit wildlife. In the spring and fall, thousands of migrating birds can be seen at the shorebird and waterfowl preserve.

Missouri River State Trail, Missouri's part of the KATY trail following the old MKT Railroad right-of-way, meanders through here, and on weekends large crowds of bikers and hikers wander along the 26 miles of trail from Highway 40 at Weldon Springs to Marthasville. If you have a bike on the roof, there is convenient parking all along the trail. There are plenty of places to eat or rent bikes if you didn't bring your own.

There's a spectacular view of the river beyond the outskirts of St. Louis on Interstate 70. There are so many good destinations along this route that you don't have to tell anyone that you are on it because you like to hug the corners and push the federally mandated speed limit to its max. This road will challenge the best Grand Prix wannabe with its collection of diamond-shaped signs warning of another set of sharp curves. But slow down and watch for wild turkey and deer. Enjoy the tidy farmhouses and pretty churches as you aim for the towns like Augusta, Dutzow, and Hermann that wait along the route.

You will enjoy Defiance's antiques shops and the Carpenter's Love, a woodworking shop right on the KATY trail. History buffs will want to take a 6-mile detour from Highway 94 down Highway F to the Daniel Boone home.

Somehow you would imagine a log cabin—or a sod hut, maybe. This beautiful stone house with ivy clinging to its double chimneys, crisply painted shutters, and ample back porch is not what you'd expect at all. ⊃**Daniel Boone's Home** at Defiance is elegant and comfortable. Add a VCR and a microwave, and you could move in tomorrow.

Here are Daniel's powder horn and his long rifles, his writing desk, and the very bed where his long career on the American frontier ended. It's a small bedchamber; the four-poster bed looks as if it were just made up with fresh sheets and a clean white counterpane, ready for the man himself to come in from a hard day of hunting, trapping, settling the frontier, and making history.

The kitchen is cozy, with low beams and a huge fireplace. Mrs. Boone's butter churn sits nearby, and you can almost see the family gathered here, waiting expectantly for that rich, yellow butter to spread on hearth-baked bread.

Tours are given daily, March through December, from 9:00 A.M. to 6:00 P.M. Call (314) 987–2221.

Leaving Defiance, you'll enter the Missouri River Valley wine region. There are more wineries along Highway 94 than anywhere else in the state. You can visit Boone Country Winery west of Defiance, Montelle Winery at Osage Ridge, Augusta Winery and Mount Pleasant Winery in Augusta, and Blumenhof Vineyards in Dutzow. All offer wine tasting and sales as well as great spots to enjoy a bottle of wine with a picnic lunch.

Just down the road a piece from Dan'ls house you'll find the little German wine-producing town of Augusta. A hundred and fifty years ago it was a self-sufficient town with a cooperage works, stores, and a German school. Before Prohibition, when Missouri was the second-largest wine-producing state in the nation, there were thirteen wineries located in Augusta's valley, beyond the bluffs above the southernmost bend of the river. Deep, well-drained soil and freedom from spring frosts were perfect for viticulture. This is recognized as America's first official wine district and the first in the New World to bear an official "Appellation Control" designation.

Augusta still deserves its reputation. ⊃**Mount Pleasant Wine Company** (314–228–4419) was purchased in 1966 by Lucian and Eva Dressel (it's now owned by MPW, Inc.). A short twenty years later, the Dressels' 1986 Vintage Port took top port honors in the International Wine and Spirit Competition in London, England, making theirs the first Missouri winery since Prohibition to win an international gold medal, from a field of 1,175 wines and more than twenty countries.

Mount Pleasant's 1987 Jour de la Victoire Ice Wine also won a silver medal, the highest award given to an American ice wine. The Cheese Wedge, on site at the winery, features products made in Missouri. Manager Rita Struckhoff says there's cheese from Emma (that's a town), sausage from Washington, and mustard from Wolf Island, Missouri. Hours are Monday through Saturday

Mount Pleasant Wine Company

from 10:00 A.M. to 5:00 P.M. and Sunday from noon to 5:30 P.M. Mount Pleasant even delivers!

Gleaming copper and brass, the work of more than thirty potters and craftspeople, greet your eyes at **Americana Galleries** (314–228–4494), a cluster of reconstructed early log buildings. Coppersmith Michael Bruckdorfer keeps random winter hours, but is open from April through Christmas on weekdays from 10:30 A.M. to 4:30 P.M., Saturdays from 10:00 A.M. to 5:00 P.M., and Sunday afternoons. The galleries are at the corner of Walnut and Ferry streets.

The town invites leisurely exploration. Stay over at the **Lindenhof Country Inn** (314–228–4617) at the corner of Walnut and Jackson; you can't miss that pink Victorian with its blue trim and ornate iron fence. The rate is $60 double occupancy per night. Other B&Bs are nearby; look around.

Fresh and rested, the next day you can wander the town to discover country stores, fudge factories, antiques shops, and a museum. Don't miss the **Cookie Jar Restaurant** and **The Bread Shed** (314–228–4536) next door; the aroma alone is enough to wake you with a smile.

If you love fine furniture with an elegant, contemporary feel, you'd hardly expect to find it in the backcountry. But at ⊃**Nona Woodworks,** furniture maker Michael Bauermeister is full of surprises. He works with Missouri woods to create delicate, finely designed pieces that would grace the best of homes. "Rita's Desk," for example, is a lovely little fall-front desk of cherry wood. The angular top is a beautiful contrast to the curved and hard-carved legs.

Michael's shop is in an old-fashioned store building in the town of Nona—which isn't a town anymore. It's just Michael's house and shop and a few other buildings. Follow Highway 47 to Augusta Bottom Road and continue on that road for 3½ miles. The shop is just 3 miles from Mt. Pleasant Winery. Shop hours are unpredictable—special orders and commissions keep the craftsman hopping. Call (314) 228–4663 to make sure your trip won't be for nothing.

For a sweet treat stop by Bob and Ellen Knoernschild's **Centennial Farms** in Augusta just off Highway 94 at 199 Jackson Street and chomp into a sweet apple from their ten-acre orchard. Most of the apples grown here end up in the sweet apple butter the Knoernschilds slow-cook and hand-stir for twelve hours in an open 50-gallon copper kettle, just the way apple butter is supposed to be made. But they have unique variations that Grandma never tried—honey, anise, and sugarless apple butters are so good on a hot biscuit. Bob and Ellen also sell cherries, strawberries, peaches, and fresh vegetables. The apple butter comes in 10- and 20-ounce jars for $1.60 and $2.65. You can mail order some, too. Call (314) 228–4338.

A one-lane bridge followed by a ninety-degree turn leads you to Dutzow. (If you found Augusta charming, Dutzow is downright quaint.) This historic Dutch town, founded in 1832 by Baron Von Bock, was the first German settlement in the Missouri River Valley. In the mid-nineteenth century "Missouri's Rhineland" attracted immigrants who were inspired by enthusiastic accounts of natural beauty and bounty; among the most convincing was Gottfried Duden's *Report on a Journey to the Western States of North America*, published in 1829, which contributed to the settlement of these lovely little enclaves all up and down the Missouri River.

The town offers several antiques shops and a pretty good sandwich at the **Dutzow Deli** in an old gas station next to the town post office. It's a popular stop along the KATY trail.

‌**Blumenhof Vineyards and Winery** (314–433–2245) takes its name from the Blumenberg family's ancestral farm in the Harz Mountains of Germany; *blumenhof* translates as "court of flowers." Enjoy the winery's Teutonic decor and the welcome invitation to stop and smell the flowers—along with the bouquet of the wine. Blumenhof produces wines from the finest American and European varietal grapes. There's a full range of wines, but dry table wines are a tour de force. (The Vidal Blanc won a gold medal in international competition.) Visit any day except Easter, Thanksgiving, Christmas, or New Year's, 10:30 A.M. to 5:30 P.M. Monday through Saturday and Sunday from noon to 5:30 P.M.

The ‌**Concord Hill Bed and Breakfast** (314–932–4228) offers city-weary guests three large bedrooms and a huge loft that comfortably sleeps five adults. Add a hot tub, wet bar, and full kitchen; it's an ideal weekend retreat for groups of up to eleven. A continental breakfast is provided and anything from elegant candlelight dinners to simple box lunches can be prearranged; now *that's* a getaway. This nineteenth-century farmhouse is in the tiny agricultural town of Concord Hill, population forty; this is definitely off the beaten path!

There is one more KATY stop at Marthasville. "Over the river and through the woods, to Grandmother's house we go. . . ." If you don't have a grandma in the country, visit **Gramma's House** (314–433–2675) near Marthasville; it's like going home. Enjoy a brisk game of horseshoes, look for a bluebird on the fence, or just skip stones in the creek. After sleeping like a stone in these peaceful surroundings, your grandma—that is, hostess—will fix you a hearty breakfast; best clean your plate. Weekend rates are $65 per couple or $50 during the week; a lovely private cottage is $75. Gramma's House is popular with trail users; make *this* Gramma's a rest stop and stay on for the comfort and the ambience.

Bluffs of the Mighty Mo

Highway 94 winds over steep hills set with ponds and quiet, picturesque farms. Small and almost picture-postcard pretty, buildings nestled in the trees are clearly visible in winter and half-hidden in summer; you'll have to look sharp. The highway follows the river through a series of tiny towns that give you a taste of Missouri past. Rhineland, Bluffton, Steedman, Mokane— each is as inviting as the last. Heads up; you may find a great little cafe here or a hidden mine of antiques.

Hikers can find their way through ⊃**Rock Bridge State Park** (314–449–7402) off Highway 63 with only a map and a compass; the University of Missouri Orienteering Club has set up a maze-like course through these wooded hills. You can't miss the huge, natural stone bridge that gives the park its name, though. This 300-million-year-old rock formation waited till the 1820s to be discovered by pioneers looking for a perfect site to mill their grain. The gristmill that once occupied the site is gone now. The little quarry nearby served as a stage for plays and chautauquas; you can still hear the echoes of the voices in the whisper of wind.

Plan to stay awhile in Columbia. It's a great base camp for some far-flung exploring—that is, once you can tear yourself away from the town itself.

Columbia is home of the University of Missouri, a beautiful campus that houses a number of disciplines. If you have an interest in antiquities, don't miss the ⊃**Museum of Art and Archaeology,** boasting a collection from six continents and five millennia. The museum, in Pickard Hall at the corner of University Avenue and Ninth Street, is on the historic Francis quadrangle. Built in 1894, it's on the National Register of Historic Places. You'll find artworks by Lyonel Feininger, Lakshmi, Francken the Younger, and many well-known classical and contemporary American artists. The museum is open 9:00 A.M. till 5:00 P.M. Tuesday through Friday and noon till 5:00 P.M. on weekends.

Archaeology has long been a strong field of study at the university, which offers B.A., M.A., and Ph.D. degrees as well as courses in museum studies. The museum's collections reflect almost a century of work by students and faculty in places as diverse as Africa, Egypt, South Asia, Greece, and the American Southwest. Pre-Columbian and Oceanic works round out the collection.

The museum is wheelchair accessible; there are tours for the visually impaired available without prior notice. Other guided tours can be arranged by calling (314) 882–3591 (at least two weeks in advance for groups).

Columbia has an active and varied crafts community. **Bluestem Missouri Crafts** (314–442–0211) showcases the work of over eighty Missouri artists and craftspeople. Whatever your particular weakness, from wrought iron to weaving, from folk-art whirligigs to fine jewelry, you'll find it at Bluestem (named after the native prairie grass, of course); the shop is located at 13 South Ninth Street. Shop 10:00 A.M. till 6:00 P.M. Monday through Saturday, until 8:30 P.M. Thursday night, and noon until 5:00 P.M. on Sunday.

Hungry? Shopping will do that to you. But like most college towns, Columbia has more restaurants and cafes than you're likely to cover if you stay for weeks—the selection is dizzying. Collar a student and ask which of the Asian restaurants is best or where to go for a romantic evening for two.

The **1909 Katy Station** at Fourth and Broadway was once a station house for the Missouri, Kansas and Texas Railroad. Now on the National Register of Historic Places, the station delivers fine dining from 11 A.M. to 10:00 P.M. Dinner entrees run from $6.00 to $15.00. Call (314) 449–0835 for reservations.

One final gustatory note—okay, two: truffles and chocolate pizza. You'll find these and too many other rich temptations to mention at **The Candy Factory,** 1016 East Broadway. These folks call themselves "your hometown candy makers," but the good news is that even if Columbia isn't your home town, they'll be glad to ship anything you want, nationwide. Use the special order number (314–443–8222). You can even buy sugar-free chocolates for those people on restricted diets who still need a treat. Prices seem moderate enough; a holiday gift basket ranges from $12 to $52.

History buffs take note: **Maplewood** is 4 miles south of Interstate 70 at the AC Exit off Highway 63. This beautiful old brick home with graceful white columns and crisply painted shutters is a rare surviving example of a late nineteenth-century rural homestead. Complete with the original hay and horse barns, a carriage house, and other outbuildings, it was placed on the National Register of Historic Places in 1979.

Maplewood contained the latest innovations when it was built in 1877 by the Slater Lenoir family. Dr. Frank and Lavinia (Lenoir) Nifong owned the home from 1905 on, and it once again became a center of activity for the Columbia area community. Dr. Lenoir practiced progressive farming techniques, some of which you may explore on site.

Through the summer months, the Maplewood Barn Theatre offers open-air performances here. For reservations or information, call (314) 449–7517. The carriage house contains the original family conveyances; you can take a trip to nineteenth-century Missouri on Sundays from 2:00 P.M. till 5:00 P.M., April through October. Call the Columbia Visitors' Bureau at (314) 875–1231 for reservations. Admission to Maplewood is by donation, so be generous. Your contributions will keep it open to the public.

Missouri's answer to the Hard Rock Cafe is just outside of Columbia at 5801 North New Highway 763—**The 63 Diner** (314–443–2331). Bright black, white, and chrome decor, dozens of photos of rock 'n' roll favorites and old movie stars, waitresses in saddle shoes and circle skirts, and the end of that big red '59 Cadillac sticking out of the front wall make the place loaded with atmosphere. The food's every bit as good as you remember, too.

About 11 miles east of Columbia on Highway WW and then some gravel roads, Patrick Nelson makes eighteenth- and nineteenth-century reproductions and architectural pieces on his small farm. Using cherry, oak, poplar, walnut, hickory—traditional woods used in American furniture—Nelson can reproduce anything you can show him a picture of, including fireplace mantels and custom molding. He makes doors, bedroom and dining room sets, Windsor chairs, and greenwood country chairs. He can alter pieces to fit modern homes or oversized customers. Call ahead for directions to his shop, which is out back in a shed on the farm. There are usually a few pieces in progress to indicate the caliber of his skill, and you can show him what you have in mind and discuss the price. Reach him at (314) 642–7776.

Follow the signs from the Rocheport exit to ⊃**Moniteau Creek Pottery** (314–698–4011). Fine handcrafted porcelain and stoneware pottery by John Preus is available in a wide variety of shapes and sizes. Find a deep, generous bowl for popcorn, a teapot for a winter's cup of warmth, jars, and more. John—or his representative—is in the shop Wednesdays, Fridays, and Saturdays from 10:00 A.M. until 5:00 P.M., or by appointment anytime.

Rocheport is a good spot to sample the KATY trail through Missouri's middle; it is among the longest of the nation's growing network of rail-trails and by 1994 will stretch 200 miles from

Machens just north of St. Louis to Sedalia 90 miles east of Kansas City. The KATY trail follows the old Missouri-Kansas-Texas Railroad bed that curves along the north bank of the Missouri River, and one of the most scenic parts of the trail rolls from Rocheport southeast to Jefferson City along a wooded band between the river and the cliffs—sheer limestone walls rising 100 feet above the Muddy Mo. The compacted rock pathway is easy riding even for thin racing tires; the canopy of oak and sycamore trees offers brilliant color in the fall, and the trail is flowered with dogwood and redbud in the spring. Summertime rides lead through kaleidoscopic colors of wildflowers and trumpet vine blossoms fluttering with hummingbirds.

Many caves are chiseled into the cliffside—in fact, on most days you can tour Boone Cave, named for Daniel Boone, who spent time in this area. It is privately owned and admission is charged, but it offers a cool spot to rest up a bit before turning back toward Rocheport. Tours of Boone Cave are given by Jim Babcock, who once lived near the cave and explored it several times a day; it's as if he invites you into his home. An expert on Rocheport history, Babcock can tell you all about the town while you're strolling along the walkways throughout the cave.

Or you may want to continue through cornfields and pastureland and small towns to the state capital at Jefferson City—about 15 more miles. Daytrips in both directions are possible from Rocheport. So far there are no camping facilities along the trail. Even if you don't plan to use the trail, you'll enjoy the many shops and restaurants that have sprung up to cater to the biking crowd.

If you want to try part of the trail, bikes can be rented at the **Trailside Cafe.** Basic bikes are $3.00 per hour or $10.00 per day. Betty Slate, owner of the cafe, has expanded the business from a simple cafe to a complete biker's rest stop. She offers a gift shop with bike accessories, a bike garage, and rental of all kinds of bicycles from training wheels on up. There are even pull-carts to tote children too young to pedal. One of the more popular bikes is the tandem bike, which rents for $5.00 per hour or $18.00 a day. The Trailside Cafe is at First and Pike streets and is open from 8:30 A.M. until 8:00 P.M. Monday through Friday and 7:00 A.M. until 8:00 P.M. on weekends until November 1. During the winter Betty opens on "pretty weekends." Call (314) 698–2702. (In Columbia, CycleSports at 1020 East Broadway

(314–875–2700) rents mountain, hybrid, and racing bikes plus helmets and child trailers for an average of $15 per day. Hourly rates are also available. Hours are Monday through Saturday 9:00 A.M. to 6:00 P.M.)

If it's not telling tales out of school, you may want to enroll for a term at the **School House Bed and Breakfast** (314–698–2022) in Rocheport. Innkeepers John and Vicki Ott have restored this big foursquare edifice at Third and Clark streets and made it more inviting than any school *we've* seen. The three-story school was built in 1914 and served as the area's cultural center for over sixty years.

There are now eight guests rooms, each with its own style; there are even antique bathtubs, sinks, and toilets. The Bridal Suite contains a heart-shaped Jacuzzi. The garden courtyard invites relaxation, and the period reception room is available for meetings, business retreats, and intimate parties. Room rates are from $55 per night and include a hearty country breakfast. Whitehorse Antiques, with ten dealers, is on the lower level of the school.

Craft and antiques shops, the Woodwoman Gallery, the New River City Theater, the Word of Mouth Cafe, and the Rocheport Museum nearby offer the visitor plenty to do "out of school."

The family-owned winery Les Bourgeois Vineyards (314–698–3401) welcomes visitors. It is located south of Rocheport on Highway BB, 1 mile north of Interstate 70. Admire a spectacular view of the Missouri River as you sample Bordeaux-style wines— plus a generous basket of Missouri sausage, cheese, and fresh fruit. Wine garden hours are noon to sunset, Monday through Saturday; Sunday noon to 6:00 P.M. from March through November, but the winery and sales room are open every day of the year from 11:00 A.M. to 6:00 P.M.

All this driving makes a body thirsty, but by now you've had enough wine; how about an old-fashioned cherry phosphate? Or maybe a thick, rich malt made with hand-dipped ice cream? Stop by tiny Glasgow, where you'll find ⊃**Henderson's,** a fifth-generation drugstore on the main drag. They'll fix you the fantasy float of your dreams.

Glasgow's narrow, two-story city hall has a surprised expression; the round-topped windows look like raised eyebrows. But there's nothing too shocking in this historic little town unless you discover that the old bridge on Highway 240 is the world's first all-steel bridge, built in 1878. Eight hundred tons of steel were used in construction at a cost of $500,000; it costs more than that to salt the wintry streets of a small city today.

Near Fayette is the only spot in the entire Western Hemisphere—that's *hemisphere*, folks—where you'll find inland salt grass. Moniteau Lick, near the more familiar Boone's Lick, is the place. This area was once important for naturally occurring salt; there are more than eighty place-names in Missouri containing the word "salt" or "saline."

Glaciated Plains

Civil War buffs will discover the General Sterling Price Monument by the highway at Keytesville. Farther north you'll pass through a real Mickey Mouse town (Marceline is the birthplace of Walt Disney) on your way to Brookfield. Every Labor Day, hot-air balloon races are held nearby. There's a sustained "swooooosh" as the balloons lift off; it sounds like the sharp intake of the watching crowd's breath, but it's the hot breath of the craft themselves, rising in the morning air. More than fifty balloons join in the fun, filling the sky with crayon-box colors.

From here, a short jaunt westward will take you to Laclede and the ⊃**General John J. Pershing Boyhood Home.** The Rural Gothic building is a National Historic Landmark and is as ramrod straight as the old man himself, softened with just a bit of gingerbread. The museum highlights Pershing's long career. Only 3 miles away is the Pershing State Park, with the largest remaining wet prairie in Missouri, Late Woodland Indian mounds, and the War Mothers Statue. Also, Locust Creek Covered Bridge State Historic Site is just north of Pershing's home.

Open farmland dominates Highway 5 North; the rolling hills recall the prairie that covered much of presettlement Missouri. Eastward, just outside of Milan discover busy **Kirksville** and environs. There's a lot happening in Kirksville, as always in a college town. This is the home of Northeast Missouri State University and the Kirksville College of Osteopathic Medicine—lots of lively young things running around here, having fun, eating out, and just generally being college kids.

Is your family doctor an M.D. or a D.O.? If he is a doctor of Osteopathy (D.O.), his profession got its start right here in

Kirksville when Andrew Taylor Still established the first school of the osteopathic profession in 1892, in a one-room school-house. The college has grown; today there are fifteen buildings (including two hospitals) on a fifty-acre campus, and the student body numbers more than 500. Former United States Surgeon General C. Everett Koop himself delivered the 1988 commencement address.

Visit the ⊃**Andrew Taylor Still National Osteopathic Museum** at 311 Fourth Street weekdays from 9:00 A.M. till 3:00 P.M. It's a three-building complex that includes the log cabin birthplace of Dr. Still, the tiny, white clapboard cabin that served as the school, and the museum itself, with its impressive collection of osteopathic paraphernalia.

Northeast Missouri State University is no slouch, either. You may have read about it in the *U.S. News and World Report* survey of "America's Best Colleges." Or, maybe you saw "Best of the Bargain Colleges" in *Kiplinger's Personal Finance Magazine,* or noted the name in *USA Today, Money,* or the *New York Times.*

If you're a scholar of Abraham Lincoln, don't miss the Schwengel Lincoln Collection on the NMSU campus. Books, personal effects, and memorabilia concerning our sixteenth president are located in the Special Collections Department of Pickler Memorial Library. The department is open between 8:00 A.M. and 5:00 P.M.

Buildings of many architectural styles, from Romanesque and Renaissance Revival to Italianate and Victorian, from Art Deco and Art Nouveau to Beaux Arts and Prairie, strut their stuff on the walking tour of Old Towne Kirksville. Begin the grand tour at Old Towne Park (Elson and Washington streets) and follow the signs, or pick up a map at any of the businesses marked with a red flag. It's only 1⅓ miles by foot—but well over a hundred years if you're traveling in time.

Tourists always gravitate to the restaurants; what's more fun than eating out? You'll like what Kirksville has to offer; as a college town it has a wide variety of eateries, including Minn's Cuisine for exotic French, Hunan, and Chinese delicacies, Bogie's for batter-fried lobster or chicken piccata, and Too-Tall's Two Eatery and Deli.

The Manhattan (816–665–2075) is the longest-established restaurant in northeast Missouri, owned by the same family for three generations. They know what they're doing—nobody stays in business that long without having something on the ball. Try the Athenian salad, gyros, eggplant parmigiana, and best of all, avgolemono soup. (If that's Greek to you, it's an egg-lemon soup that may sound strange but is heaven to the taste buds.) While we're speaking Greek, don't forget a tiny slice of baklava, that phyllo pastry, honey, and nut confection that really is "food for the gods." Hours are 11:00 A.M. to 8:00 P.M. on Sunday and 11:00 A.M. to 9:00 P.M. Tuesday through Saturday.

When the night life gets too much for you in hoppin' Kirksville, head out of town to ⊃**Thousand Hills State Park.** This part of Missouri was sculpted by glaciers; rich, glacial soil is the norm, not the exception, and the streams and rivers that cut through this deep soil formed the "thousand hills."

The park straddles the Grand Divide. Like the Continental Divide, this geologic land form is an area where high ground determines the direction of surface water drainage. It always seems as if you should feel the difference as you cross, but you don't. This mini-mountain ridge runs along Highway 63 from the Iowa-Missouri border to just south of Moberly; western streams and rivers flow into the Missouri River, eastern waters into the Mississippi.

Much of the park is remnant prairie—look for big bluestem, rattlesnake master, blazing star, and Indian grass, which are maintained by periodic burning. Because of the cooler climate here, you'll find plants not found in other parts of the state, such as the lovely interrupted fern in the deep ravines in the park. There is a natural grove of large-toothed aspen, a tree common to northern states but quite rare in Missouri. In Thousand Hills State Park you can find our grand-champion aspen.

If prehistory interests you more than natural history, don't miss the petroglyphs near camping area No.3. Archaeologists believe these crosses, thunderbirds, sunbursts, and arrows were scratched into the native sandstone by peoples who inhabited the site between A.D 1000 and 1600. They may have been reminders of the order of the ceremonial rituals passed along by the Middle Mississippi culture, which were in use for a long period of time. Many glyphs appear to have been carved by hunters of the Late Woodland culture between A.D. 400 and 900. The site is listed on the National Register of Historic Places; it's nice to know this list contains more than the usual antebellum mansions and federal-style courthouses we seem to expect.

Take the highway south to Ethel—that is, if you love hand-thrown pottery. This little town is the home of Clay Images (816–486–3471). Jim and Melissa Hogenson are well-known artists who work in clay; you may have seen their whimsies—dragons and wizards—at Renaissance festivals around the country. Don't miss this little gold mine (all right, clay mine).

Tiny Ten Mile just north of Macon doesn't even show on the map; it's an Amish community near Ethel. Watch for little yard signs; many of these places have tiny shops on the farmstead where baked goods, yard goods, homemade candy, and baskets or quilts are sold.

Take the grand tour through Paris (no, not the long way around; this is Paris, Missouri) to tiny Florida, the closest town to the ꓽ**Mark Twain Birthplace State Historic Site** (314–565–3449) and Mark Twain State Park, which offers camping, swimming, and river recreation. The two-room cabin where Samuel Clemens came into the world reminds you of something; it could have come straight from one of his books. A bit of Twain *was* Tom Sawyer and Huck Finn (you remember Huck, that red-haired scamp who lived life to the hilt, devil-take-the-hindmost). If you've read *The Adventures of Huckleberry Finn,* this won't come as a big surprise.

What *is* a surprise is that the two-room cabin is totally enclosed in an ultramodern museum, which houses first editions of Clemens's works, including the handwritten version of *Tom Sawyer* done for British publication. Sit in the public reading room to conduct personal research—or just to get in touch with the old wag. For example, Twain once wrote, "Recently someone in Missouri has sent me a picture of the house I was born in. Heretofore I always stated that it was a palace but I shall be more guarded now." Admission is $2.00 for adults, $1.25 for children six to twelve, and free for under six. Special group rates are available.

Also, the second full weekend of August each year the Corps of Engineers, the Missouri Department of Natural Resources, and the Friends of Florida sponsor the Salt River Folklife Festival in the tiny town of Florida.

Five miles west of Paris and 3 miles south on County Route C, you'll find a different kind of nostalgic symbol, the Union Covered Bridge. You can almost hear the clatter of horses' hooves and the rumble of wagon wheels through the old wooden tunnel. (You'll have to use your imagination; the recently restored bridge is open to foot traffic only; it's blocked to vehicles.) A set of inter-pretive displays at the unmanned site fill you in on covered bridge history in Missouri. Call the Mark Twain Birthplace at (314) 565–3449 for information and directions to the bridge.

There are some pretty exotic destinations around here, aren't there? Milan, Paris—and now Mexico, south of "gay Paree." Mexico is called "Little Dixie," because of its strong southern sympa-thies during the Civil War; now you can visit the Little Dixie Wildlife Area nearby.

Notice all the red brick buildings in the Mexico/Vandalia area? The land is underlaid with a type of refractory clay that makes great bricks; there are still four brick plants in Audrain County.

A 14-mile jog back east from Mexico will take you to Centralia. Don't miss it if you enjoy "kinder, gentler" countryside. ⊃**Chance Gardens** includes a turn-of-the-century mansion, home of the late A. Bishop Chance. Build in 1904, that onion-domed turret, gracious porticoes, and ornate woodwork invite visitors with an eye for elegance. A gift to the public from the A. B. Chance Company (the town's largest industry), it's been Centralia's showplace for years.

The gardens that surround the home say something about the kind of luxury money can't buy. It takes time to plan those masses of color that bloom continuously through the seasons and lead the eye from one brilliant display to another—time to plan and time to maintain. That's a luxury most of us don't have.

Tiny Clark, a hoot and a holler from Centralia, is the birth-place of General Omar Bradley. There's an active Amish commu-nity in the Clark area; watch for those horses and buggies. Some sport bumper stickers, much easier to read at this speed than on the interstates. I'M NOT DEAF, I'M IGNORING YOU and I MAY BE SLOW, BUT I'M AHEAD OF YOU seem to be local favorites. You'll want to slow down yourself to admire the clean, white homes and com-modious barns of the Amish.

Missouri's Monarchy

Just before you hit Interstate 70 Highway 54 South, you enter the ⊃**Kingdom of Callaway.** Did you hear that right? Indeed you did. This is a separate kingdom, with occasional royalty in attendance. It's a long story that has become legend over the years; who you believe depends on who you want to believe. It's a great tale, in any case.

During the Civil War a small band of hometown irregulars (boys and old men, mostly) was about to be overrun by vastly superior Union forces. To prevent the kind of disaster that had happened elsewhere, Colonel Jefferson F. Jones, representing the people of Callaway County, negotiated a treaty. Union General John B. Henderson agreed not to invade the county, and Jones agreed to disband his men. Of course, to hear the home boys tell it, the Union agreed to the truce to avoid conflict with the fierce locals who had bolstered their imaginary forces with several black-painted "cannons" made of fallen logs.

Since Jones acted independently and not as an official government representative, the "Kingdom of Callaway" came into being. It was a kind of secession within a secession, and somehow "the Kingdom" (Callaway County) never quite got around to officially rejoining the rest of us. With a kind of tongue-in-cheek good humor, residents celebrate their independence and flaunt the monarchy at every opportunity. You can bet the IRS still gets their cash, though.

You'll notice little Kingdom City here, not exactly what you'd expect as a seat of power—but then, it isn't. Fulton is the county seat, a charming town of cobblestone streets, historic buildings, and Victorian lighting fixtures. It is steeped in international history as well.

For starters, Fulton has played host to Winnie—that's Winston Churchill—who journeyed here to address Westminster College in 1946. Churchill was out of office when he delivered the most famous speech of his life, the "Iron Curtain" speech. "From Stettin in the Baltic to Trieste in the Adriatic, an iron curtain has descended across the Continent. Behind that line lie all the capitals of the ancient states of Central and Eastern Europe. . . ." Those were prophetic words; what would Churchill say now?

The ties between the college, the town, and Great Britain remain unbroken. In the 1960s, Westminster President R. L. D. Davidson wanted to honor those ties. The resulting plan was bold and perfect—if not as well-publicized as the move of the London Bridge to Arizona. The college acquired the Church of St. Mary the Virgin, Aldermanbury, England, and dismantled it stone by stone. The edifice was shipped across the Atlantic and cross-country to Fulton, where it was reconstructed on

Westminster campus and rededicated in 1969. It now houses the ⊃**Winston Churchill Memorial and Library** (314–642–3361 or –6648), currently the only center in the United States dedicated to the study of the man and his works. Churchill's original oil paintings (the very public man had a private side, and enjoyed relaxing with his paints), letters, manuscripts, personal family mementoes, and other memorabilia are on display, in addition to the fire-scarred communion plate rescued from the ruins of the church after World War II.

The church itself is deeply historical; built in twelfth-century London, it was redesigned in 1677 by Sir Christopher Wren, one of the finest architects of the period. Damage caused by German bombs seemed to signal its end until Westminster College stepped in to rescue the building. It is open from 10:00 A.M. to 4:30 P.M. seven days a week. Admission is $2.50; $2.00 for AAA members and senior citizens. Children twelve and under are free.

There is a memorial of a different kind in the same town: the **George Washington Carver Memorial** at 909 Westminster Avenue (314–642–5551) honors the Diamond, Missouri, native and presents information about one of our greatest humanitarians and scientists. The memorial includes a study of black history in Missouri as well. It is open on weekends, and admission is $1.00.

The **Loganberry Inn** (314–642–9229), a turn-of-the-century Victorian home, offers guests B&B accommodations at 310 West Seventh Street, only a block from Westminster College. Rates are from $50 to $60.

Fulton was also the home of Henry Bellamann, author of *King's Row*. Set in Fulton, the novel was made into a movie in the 1940s starring none other than Missourian Bob Cummings and a pre-presidential Ronald Reagan. The chamber of commerce displays memorabilia from the movie and offers a walking tour of the *King's Row* setting. (There is a temptation to joke about Reagan's later reign, isn't there?)

Thence, hie thyself back east along Interstate 70 to ⊃**Graham Cave State Park** (314–564–3476) near Danville. (Oops, this royalty stuff gets to you!) This rainbow-shaped sandstone cave is shallow, so the tour is a self-guided one. Spelunkers, don't let that put you off. Although this is not a deep-earth cave with spectacular formations, artifacts were found here dating from the area's earliest human habitation, some 10,000 years ago. Before the Native Americans formed themselves into tribes, Graham

Cave was an important gathering place. Spear-type flints, made before the bow was invented, were found here, along with other signs of human use. Admire these fine examples of the earliest Show-Me State inhabitants in the small museum in the park office. Take the Danville/Montgomery City exit off the interstate and follow Outer Road TT 2 miles west; it dead-ends at the park, so you can't go wrong.

INDEX

Index

Index